CANADIAN OBSESSIONS

CANADIAN OBSESSIONS

A CENTURY OF NATIONAL PREOCCUPATIONS, AS SEEN BY MACLEAN'S

EDITED BY
PAMELA YOUNG

DOUGLAS & McINTYRE
VANCOUVER / TORONTO

Douglas & McIntyre Ltd.
2323 Quebec Street, Suite 201
Vancouver, British Columbia
V5T 4S7
www.douglas-mcintyre.com

Library and Archives Canada Cataloguing in Publication

Canadian obsessions : a century of national preoccupations, as seen by
Maclean's / edited by Pamela Young.

ISBN 1-55365-097-2

1. Canada—History—20th century—Pictorial works. 2. Canada—History—20th
century. I. Young, Pamela, 1960-

FC600.C317 2005   971'.0022'2   C2004-907346-X

Editing by Pamela Young
Photo editing and design by Janice Van Eck
Front cover photograph from the *Maclean's* archives
Typesetting by Janice Van Eck
Printed and bound in Canada by Friesens
Printed on acid-free paper

We gratefully acknowledge the financial support of the Canada Council for
the Arts, the British Columbia Arts Council, and the Government of Canada
through the Book Publishing Industry Development Program (BPIDP) for our
publishing activities.

CONTENTS

INTRODUCTIONS

The first person to think about making *Maclean's* into a weekly newsmagazine was Lt.-Col. John Bayne Maclean—the same man who, in 1905, launched a monthly known in its early days as *Busy Man's Magazine*. In the century since, *Maclean's*, as it was renamed in 1911, has been a business magazine, a general interest magazine, and a magazine that published fiction, art, and, on occasion, poetry. In 1978, thanks to publisher Lloyd Hodgkinson and editor Peter C. Newman, it fulfilled Maclean's vision and became a weekly newsmagazine.

Maclean's has always provided a window through which Canadians could look to and at each other, and chart the country's progress. We often say the past shapes our present, but the reverse is equally true: we constantly reshape the significance of previous events to better suit our present-day wishes. That's why photographs and reports of events, recounted in the magazine shortly after they occurred, are so compelling. They provide flash-frozen evidence of how situations appeared at the time, before hindsight and reinterpretation retouched them—for example, what is now known as The First World War was, in its immediate aftermath, called The War to End All Wars. And it's refreshing to realize that each generation thinks it has cornered the market on technology and modernity: in 1909, when Canada's first documented airplane flight occurred, it seemed every bit as breathtaking— or even more so—than does Canadian participation in space exploration today.

We've deliberately avoided using the word "history" in the title of this book. *Canadian Obsessions* is not a history of Canada, and it's not a history of *Maclean's* either: rather, it's a look at how the magazine portrayed people and events of the past 100 years. It's thematic rather than chronological—a non-linear approach can better measure a nation's successes, failures, shared desires and points of conflict, along with its changing attitudes and aspirations.

This book is the direct result of the hands-on work of Pamela Young, who edited it, and Janice Van Eck, its photo editor and designer; various members of *Maclean's* editorial staff who provided contributions; and Scott McIntyre and the staff of Douglas & McIntyre, its publishers. In addition to them, special thanks and credit are due to Paul Jones, publisher of *Maclean's* from 1999 to November 2004, whose enthusiasm and encyclopedic knowledge drove the project in early stages; Rachael MacKenzie, director of marketing until late last year for Rogers Publishing Limited, which publishes magazines including *Maclean's*; and the magazine's art director, Donna Braggins. Most of all, it is intended as a gesture of affection and appreciation from the magazine to its most important constituency of all—the millions of readers, past and present, who have made *Maclean's* a regular part of their lives and of the national conversation for a century. This book gives you something else to talk about: thanks for making it possible.
ANTHONY WILSON-SMITH EDITOR, *MACLEAN'S* (2001-2005)

1 2 3 4 5 6 7 8 9 10 11 12 13 14 15 16 17 18 19 20 21 22 23 24 25 26 27
54 55 56 57 58 59 60 61 62 63 64 65 66 67 68 69 70 71 72 73 74 75 76

You are handed a jigsaw puzzle box containing thousands of pieces; you don't know what the end result will look like, but you do know that only a few of the pieces will ultimately fit together to complete the puzzle. That's one analogy for how this centennial book came to be.

Actually, it began with a show in Toronto's 2003 Contact photography festival. Curated by Catherine Dean and Tracy Doyle, *The Maclean's Collection: Pictures from a Golden Age* featured photos from 1905 to 1975. It drew attention to the incredible imagery in the magazine's archives— dramatic, evocative, historic, amusing, inexplicable. *Canadian Obsessions* revisits 100 topics that have preoccupied Canadians for all or part of *Maclean's* first 100 years. Illustrations, covers and editorial cartoons are as much a part of the book's mix as photography. Some of the prints we liked best emerged dog-eared and overlaid with crop marks after decades of obscurity in the archives; they are reproduced here in this interestingly damaged state.

The bylines of Stephen Leacock, Pierre Berton, June Callwood, Peter C. Newman, Douglas Coupland and other prominent writers associated with *Maclean's* appear in this book. But *Canadian Obsessions* is very much a visually driven project: if we couldn't find compelling imagery in the archives, we dropped a topic from the lineup. (That's why there's nothing in here on, say, Meech Lake.) This book includes photographs by Yousuf Karsh and Deborah Samuel, cover illustrations by A.J. Casson and Franklin Arbuckle, and cartoons by Aislin (a.k.a. Terry Mosher) and Duncan Macpherson. It was exciting to find such wonderful material; it was depressing to see how the paper the magazine was printed on in the mid-20th century is now crumbling to dust.

Assembling *Canadian Obsessions* has been an intensely collaborative process. Photo editor and designer Janice Van Eck and I developed this book in tandem, and we've received invaluable advice and support from many people at *Maclean's*. Janice and I would like to express our gratitude to everyone Anthony Wilson-Smith acknowledges on the opposite page, and we'd also like to thank Tony himself for his unwavering support of this project.

In the course of our research we found all sorts of treasures and curiosities—W.J. Mather's vivid account of drought-fleeing Saskatchewan farm families in 1931, embarking on "the greatest internal migration Canada has seen"; Rex Woods' satirical 1954 "flag debate" cover (published more than a decade before Canada finally raised a flag of its own); a 1980 "People" page photo of a very young Wayne Gretzky modelling GWG jeans. Those first two are in this book (Obsessions 11 and 39). The last one isn't. Hockey, it seems, is Canada's No. 1 obsession— we found more inclusion-worthy images in that category than we could possibly use.

All the best to *Maclean's* on this significant birthday. I hope the material we chose conveys the unique scope of the magazine's first century.
PAMELA YOUNG
EDITOR, *CANADIAN OBSESSIONS*

30 31 32 33 34 35 36 37 38 39 40 41 42 43 44 45 46 47 48 49 50 51 52 53
79 80 81 82 83 84 85 86 87 88 89 90 91 92 93 94 95 96 97 98 99 100

TIMELINE

PUBLISHING HISTORY

1905 Lt.-Col. John Bayne MacLean, publisher of *The Canadian Grocer* and other trade titles, acquires a Toronto advertising agency's house journal and renames it *The Business Magazine.* Six years and a few name changes later, it becomes *MacLean's* (and later still, *Maclean's,* after Maclean lower-cases the "L" in his name)

HISTORY OF THE NAME

1905 *The Business Magazine*
1905 *The Busy Man's Magazine*
1905 *Busy Man's Magazine*
1911 *MacLean's Magazine*
1931 *Maclean's*

Maclean's founder Lt.-Col. John Bayne Maclean

1910 After five straight years of losses, the magazine turns its first profit ($1,923.57)
1915-1933 Horace T. Hunter, vice president, Maclean Publishing Company
1933-1952 Horace T. Hunter, president and CEO, Maclean Publishing Company
1945 Maclean Publishing Company becomes The Maclean-Hunter Publishing Company
1950 Death of John Bayne Maclean

DECEMBER
BUSY MAN'
MAGAZINE
Christmas Number

EDITORS AND WRITERS

1905 W.A. Craick, editor
1910 Craick resigns as editor. Over the next three years, others, including George B. van Blaricom and Roy Fry, will succeed him for relatively short terms. The names of Craick and his earliest successors never appear on the magazine's masthead
1913 Frank Mackenzie Chapman becomes the first editor credited as such on the masthead

1914-1920 Thomas B. Costain, editor (he later becomes the author of best-selling historical novels such as *The Black Rose)*
1915 Stephen Leacock's first byline in the magazine
1920-1926 Vernon McKenzie, editor
1926-1944 H. Napier Moore, editor
1935-1960 Beverley Baxter's "London Letter" appears regularly; his 1937 column "Why Edward Quit" (on the resignation of King

Edward VIII) is so popular it has to be reprinted
1944 *Maclean's* publishes Lionel Shapiro's gripping, eye-witness account of D-Day
1944-1949 William Arthur Irwin, editor
1947 Pierre Berton joins staff as assistant editor; his subsequent posts in the 1950s include associate editor and managing editor; he returns for half a year as contributing editor in 1963

1948-1951 W.O. Mitchell, fiction editor
1949-1960 Ralph Allen, editor
1951 Ottawa editor Blair Fraser discloses that the late Prime Minister Mackenzie King was a practicing spiritualist for the last 25 years of his life
1956 Peter C. Newman joins staff as assistant editor
1958 Peter Gzowski joins staff as assistant editor
1960-1962 Blair Fraser, editor

1962 Robert Fulford joins staff as reviews editor (later articles editor and staff writer)
1962-1964 Ken Lefolii, editor
1964 General interest magazines' share of ad revenue continues to decline. *Maclean's* youthful editorial staff is increasingly at odds with Maclean Hunter's senior publishing executives. Lefolii, 35, resigns; Gzowski, Fulford and others quit in solidarity. (Newman had already departed.)

ART DIRECTION AND IMAGERY

1905-1912 The first issue of *The Business Magazine* (later *Maclean's*) is a pocketbook-size publication with a blue cardboard cover. The cover's colour and typography change frequently in the early years, and the magazine's size increases slightly
SEPTEMBER 1913 First major redesign. The magazine's size

increases to 8 ¾" x 11"; future Group of Seven member Arthur Lismer creates a series of covers
1915 Political cartoons by Lou Skuce begin appearing in the magazine; Skuce will remain a contributor into the 1930s
1919 Size of the magazine increases to 11" x 14.4"
1929-1933 Frank Matteson Sperry, art editor; his successors include Hilton Hassell (1943) and D.M. Battersby (1944-1950)

1950-1962 Eugene Aliman, art director; he commissions cover paintings from Franklin Arbuckle, Rex Woods, Duncan Macpherson, and many other notable artists
1961-1965 Don Newlands, photo editor
1962-1963 Allan Fleming, designer of the CN logo, art editor
1963-1965 Ralph Tibbles, art director
1965-1968 Desmond English, art director

STATS AND MISCELLANY

OCTOBER 1905 Published monthly; 5,000 subscribers. A digest of non-fiction and fiction reprinted from U.S. and British magazines
NOVEMBER 1905 Publishes its first commissioned article: a profile of Senator George Fulford, the patent-medicine millionaire behind Dr. Williams' Pink Pills for Pale People. Over the next several

years, the magazine evolves from a second-run digest into a general interest publication that carries first-run articles and short stories. This mix remains essentially unchanged until the late 1950s, when the magazine stops running fiction on a regular basis
1917 Seriously in the red after a brief flirtation with profitability, *Maclean's* reduces its cover price; the tone of the magazine's

SUBSCRIBERS

Year	Subscribers
1905	5,000
1929	155,587
1939	279,986
1952	423,951
2004	400,029

coverage of politicians and military officials managing the First World War shifts from laudatory to critical
1918 As The Great War draws to a close, *Maclean's* once again becomes profitable
1923 Rival U.S. general interest magazines make inroads in Canada; *Maclean's* halves its cover price to remain competitive
1928 *Maclean's* asks its readers to choose the greatest living

"Pink Soap Princess"—By Elisabeth Sanxay
Maclean
Canada's ...ation
August 1st, 1936

1954 *Maclean's* makes a record profit ($462,000)
1957 TV's popularity is increasing; ad revenue for general interest magazines is declining. *Maclean's* posts its first loss ($170,000) in 15 years
1966 *Maclean's* posts a loss of $700,000
1970-1982 Lloyd M. Hodgkinson, publisher of *Maclean's*
1982-1992 Jim Miller, publisher of *Maclean's*

1992-1999 Brian Segal, publisher of *Maclean's*
1994 Rogers Communications [Edward S. (Ted) Rogers, president and CEO] acquires Maclean Hunter Ltd; *Maclean's* and other Maclean Hunter publications are later combined with Rogers' existing radio and TV operations to form Rogers Media Inc.
1999- Brian Segal, president and CEO, Rogers Publishing

1999-2004 Paul Jones, publisher of *Maclean's*
2004- Marc Blondeau named Rogers senior vice president, consumer publishing group, which includes *Maclean's*
2005 *Maclean's* celebrates its 100th anniversary

Left to right: December 1908 cover; March 28, 1959 Maurice Richard cover by Franklin Arbuckle; Rogers Communications president and CEO Edward S. (Ted) Rogers

Borden Spears, 51, becomes the next editor
1969 Charles Templeton becomes editor and departs within a few months
1970 Peter Gzowski becomes editor and departs within a few months
1971-1981 Peter C. Newman, editor
1975-2002 Allan Fotheringham, back-page columnist
1977-2004 Barbara Amiel, columnist

1981-1993 Kevin Doyle, editor
1988- Mary Janigan, columnist
1991- *Maclean's* publishes its first ranking of Canadian universities in 1991; Ann Dowsett Johnston oversees the annual rankings issue 1992 to the present. She edits the annual *Maclean's Guide to Canadian Universities* from 1996 to the present
1993-2001 Robert Lewis, editor
2001-2005 Anthony Wilson-Smith, editor

2003- Paul Wells, back-page columnist

This row, left to right: "London Letter" writer Beverley Baxter; journalist Sidney Katz

Below, left to right: detail from May 1, 1943 cover by A.J. Casson; illustrator Franklin Arbuckle; detail from Nov. 3, 1962 cover designed by Allan Fleming

1965-1970 Horst Ehricht, photo editor and photo director
1968-1972 Jon Eby, art director
1969 Formerly tabloid size, the magazine is relaunched in a 8″ x 11″ format
1970 First cartoon in *Maclean's* by Aislin (Terry Mosher); he will become cartoon editor in 2002
MID-1970s Ralph Tibbles returns briefly as art director; his successors include Paul Galer, Peter Christopher, and Andrew Smith

COVER PRICE

1905	20	cents
1916	15	cents
1920	20	cents
1926	10	cents
1934	**5**	cents

1979-1993 Brian Willer, chief photographer
1980-2000 Nick Burnett, art director
1990-2001 Peter Bregg, photo editor
2001- Peter Bregg, chief [staff] photographer
2001- Donna Braggins, art director; she cites Allan Fleming's work for the magazine in the early 1960s as an inspiration for her 2001 redesign

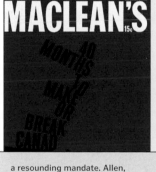

FREQUENCY

1905	monthly
1920	bi-monthly
1967	monthly
1975	bi-weekly
1978	weekly

Canadian. The winner: insulin co-discoverer Dr. Frederick G. Banting
1929 When the stock market crashes in October, *MacLean's* is profitable
1934 Revenue declines sharply in the early years of the Great Depression
1929 Issues averaged 58-100 pages in the late 1920s; the count drops to as low as 40 pages per issue in the 1930s, but circulation increases throughout the decade

1943	10 cents
1952	15 cents
1966	20 cents
1969	35 cents
1972	50 cents
1980	$1.00
1992	$2.50
1997	$3.95
2004	$4.95

1953 Sidney Katz's article, "My 12 hours as a madman," chronicles his hallucinatory experiences after taking LSD (as part of research experiments for the treatment for schizophrenia)
1957 In an editorial that goes to print in its first print in the tabulation of votes in a federal election, editor Ralph Allen writes about a Liberal victory as if it had already been confirmed. Instead, John Diefenbaker's Conservatives win

a resounding mandate. Allen, in his next editorial, describes his pre-election presumption as "an almost unexampled case of editorial fatheadedness"
1975 Ceases to be a general-interest magazine and is relaunched as a newsmagazine
1987 Excerpt from Barbara Amiel's column, following an election in the UK: "Britain has what Canada needs, Margaret Thatcher, the irreplaceable

statesman of the 20th century and, possibly, the 21st"
2001 *Maclean's* 9/11 issue (dated Sept. 24, 2001) runs without any advertising and is the first regular issue in the magazine's history devoted to a single subject

This row: detail from Aug. 1, 1936 cover by F. Sands Brunner

PERIOD PIECES

How embarrassing. In 1970, *Maclean's* ran an article saying that "plastic is now the substance of our most beautiful objects"—accompanied by a photo of a room in which everything was made of that synthetic material, including furniture, art, even the clothes the models wore. Three decades later, instead of becoming a decor staple, most plastic "art" is now on display at your local flea market.

Hard as it is to believe, that's not the only article in the archives that seems dated. Flip through 100 years worth of magazine pages and you're bound to ask yourself at least once or twice, "What were they thinking?" There are fashion spreads with women wearing a different coloured stocking on each leg, advice about what to do if someone passes you a joint at a party and precise calculations of the damage an atomic bomb would cause if dropped on the Winnipeg intersection of Portage and Main. At times, though, we were more than just naive or paranoid. Racial intolerance reared its head—"British Columbia wants to remain a white man's country for all time, and in the interest of Canada as a whole it is vitally important that she should," states one particularly disturbing *Maclean's* story from 1930 on Asian immigration to the West Coast.

That sort of comment now comes as a shock, but in many other regards we can recognize ourselves in the pages of magazines past. Aren't we always looking for the next "plastic" to fill our homes with? Who doesn't want to be ahead of the curve when it comes to fashion? While few people flinch at the mention of pot anymore, you might well ask yourself, "What should I do?" if your host were to pass you a hit of crystal meth. And the fear of terrorism has picked up where atomic bombs left off. Of course, some of our contemporary interests, concerns and fashions will also look mighty foolish 100 years from now.

Still, the majority of what has been written in the past century does stand the test of time. After all, writers, editors and readers of yesteryear and today share a preoccupation with the future. We desire to be in the know and on the ground floor of the next big thing. We fear that the worst is yet to come. And then we put our hopes in science and technology to save us.

During the Second World War, writers conjured up a tricked-out sci-fi world waiting in the wings, complete with mobile phones, fax machines and personal auto-piloted "air flivvers" for day-to-day travel. Since then, we've seen many of these things not only come to fruition but take over our lives. And we're still pining for more—or in some cases for the same things as our forebears. Really, who wouldn't want to be the first in the neighbourhood to have an air flivver? In fact, who wouldn't don two different coloured stockings if that look came back in style? Maybe asking, "What were they thinking?" is a bit harsh, when in many cases, we would have liked to have thought of it first.

SHANDA DEZIEL (SENIOR EDITOR; JOINED *MACLEAN'S* STAFF IN 1998)

1 2 3 4 5 6 7 8 9 10 11 12 13 14 15 16 17 18 19 20 21 22 23 24 25 26 27
54 55 56 57 58 59 60 61 62 63 64 65 66 67 68 69 70 71 72 73 74 75 76

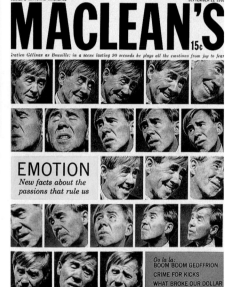

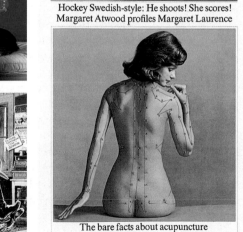

MACLEAN'S
NOVEMBER 15, 1943

O'LEE

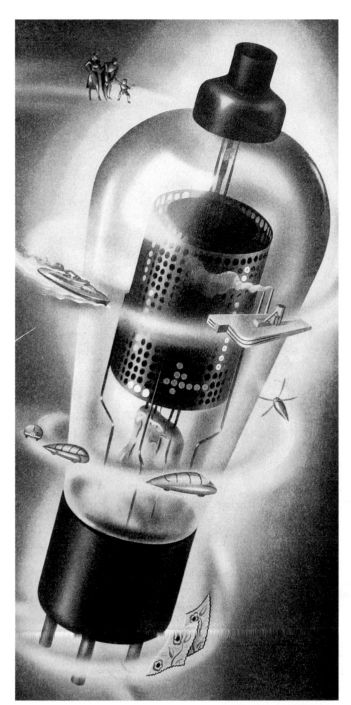

FUTURE PAST

"ELECTRON MAGIC" ILLUSTRATION
Dec. 15, 1943

Opposite page
"PLANES OF TOMORROW" ILLUSTRATION
Nov. 15, 1943

In the dark days of the Second World War, articles forecasting a bright technofuture were plentiful. The illustration on this page ran with a 1943 story that was only a few decades off with its prediction that mobile phones and fax machines would be commonplace by 1955. As for the auto-pilot "air flivvers" promised in the article excerpted at right, we're still waiting for those.

Travel by air will become . . . as commonplace as travel by automobile, train or ocean liner in the past.

But only a few have, as yet, grasped the fact that their own lives will be deeply affected by this extension of everyday travel from the earth's surface to the limitless skies.

What is it likely to mean to you, an average Canadian?

It will mean, ultimately, that you will own an air flivver, probably of the helicopter type, and you will use it as a matter of routine, just as you have used a car in the past. . . .

The flier will no longer have to be a navigator, radio operator and skilful pilot. Push-buttons will do the job.

Your aged grandmother or your teen-age son will set the airplane dials to the name or number of the city they are aiming at, start the machine, switch on the "automatic pilot," and let the plane take care of itself.

—"Planes of tomorrow," by Maj. Alexander P. de Seversky, Nov. 15, 1943

2

PLASTIC

"THE PLASTICIZATION OF PRACTICALLY EVERYTHING"
Maclean's article, February 1970

Plastic objects get their colour when they are made and never have to be painted—merely washed. . . .

A wide variety of raw materials including cotton linters (short fibres), soybeans, skim milk, air, coal and wood pulp may be made into plastics. Apparently it is pretty much a matter of what the chemists in the laboratories have on hand at the time.

—"Your house of tomorrow," by Creighton Peet, Sept. 15, 1943

The whole *world* is turning plastic. Look around. Reviled, despised plastic— so disparaged that "plastic" has become the young-generation's most pejorative word—is now the substance of our society's most beautiful objects.

The very best of our designers are showing us just what can be done with plastic, in everything from chess sets to chesterfields. Everything in this photograph (everything inanimate, that is) is plastic.

—"The plasticization of practically everything," by Marjorie Harris, February 1970

In a 1943 article on homes of the future, Creighton Peet predicted that plastic materials would become "pretty important in your house by 1955." All the same, he didn't think the proliferating plastics of his era would ever replace more conventional materials such as wood, glass and steel. But for one brief shiny moment, plastics threatened to do just that. *Maclean's*, which flirted with covering fashion, decor and other lifestyle subjects in the late '60s and early '70s, recorded the aesthetic apotheosis of synthetic polymeric substances.

The Plasticization Of Practically Everything

"Lemme give ya one word of advice," the businessman said to Dustin Hoffman in *The Graduate*. A long pause, then: "Plastics."

He may have been right. The whole *world* is turning plastic. Look around. Reviled, despised plastic — so disparaged that "plastic" has become the young-generation's most pejorative word — is now the substance of our society's most beautiful objects.

The very best of our designers are showing us just what can be done with plastic, in everything from chess sets to chesterfields. Everything in this photograph (everything inanimate, that is) is plastic. Today's slinkiest clothes have "wet-look" surfaces. The secret: designers are using plastic with honesty, not as fakery.

But one problem with plastics is that the molds are enormously expensive. A simple high chair designed by Vell Hubel, for instance, cost $12,000 for the mold alone. So high chairs require a huge volume of sales to be economically feasible. But, as the demand for elegant plastic goods increases — as it will — prices will go down. Right now the only good designs selling cheaply are inflatables. And yet, the first piece of great molded furniture was a chair designed by Charles Eames in 1948. But it took furniture manufacturers seven years to figure out how to copy it. Until very recently, they've been content to make plastic look like something else (often wood) instead of working with it to reveal its own beauties and strengths. Now, thank goodness, designers are producing plastic artifacts that are truly of our time, the antiques of the future. We've shown a few of these Canadian designs here. Turn to page 62 for a where-to-buy guide. □

PRODUCED BY MARJORIE HARRIS / PHOTOGRAPHS BY KENNETH CRAIG

3

FEAR

IF ATOMIC WAR COMES...
Maclean's article, Oct. 15, 1947

Opposite page
BRITISH GAS MASK
Maclean's editorial page, Sept. 1, 1936

Halifax, Sydney-Glace Bay and Saint John would be destroyed.... Montreal and Toronto are too large for complete destruction by a single bomb but their vital central areas would be gutted. Ottawa and Hull would become blackened ruins....

Winnipeg would be hit rather harder than any other Canadian city. It lies round and flat. Most of its homes are frame structures.... Apart from the 40,000 dead and 60,000 injured ... there would be another 200,000 or more homeless to care for, probably in midwinter.

—"If atomic war comes," by Wallace Goforth, Oct. 15, 1947

At right, a 1947 rendering of "what an atomic bomb over the corner of Portage and Main could do to Winnipeg." Opposite, from a 1936 editorial on the growing threat of war in Europe, Britain's new official civilian gas mask.

By WALLACE GOFORTH

IF YOU are among the 27% of Canadians who live in cities of over 50,000 people, or in smaller but equally vital atomic targets, then these words are written especially for you. But even if you are fortunate enough to be living on the farm, or in an ordinary small town or village, they will greatly concern your future, even though they do not directly affect the safety of your life.

You have never seen an atomic bomb; you hope you never will. You have heard about five such bombs—exploded in New Mexico, Japan and near a remote South Sea island called Bikini. You know that only two of these bombs actually brought death and destruction to great cities.

Now one great nation is making atomic bombs as fast as it can and half a dozen other nations are trying to find out how to make them. Meanwhile the politicians are struggling to find some method of preventing this deadly menace from being let loose on the world.

What does all this mean to the average Canadian? What can we or should we do about the menace of the bomb?

In my view, until all nations permanently renounce force and violence in any form as a means for settling their differences and disputes, we in Canada cannot afford to ignore defense against the atom bomb until the danger of its use is imminent. If we allow the years to roll by with only a chosen few in the armed services, in government and in scientific laboratories—like those at Chalk River—to think and plan our safety, then we will be too late to do anything about it.

Even if four out of five—or nine out of 10—enemy aircraft loaded with atomic bombs were intercepted and destroyed before they could reach their targets, it would only require 25 such aircraft out of 250 to break through and drop their super-lethal eggs over a selection of Canadian cities. The enemy's objective would then be attained, as far as this country is concerned.

The only province left untouched by this potential attacking wave of the future would be Prince Edward Island. The Maritime cities of Halifax, Sydney-Glace Bay and Saint John would be destroyed. So would Quebec City, Shipshaw, Arvida, and Shawinigan Falls. Montreal and Toronto are too large for complete destruction by a single bomb but their vital central areas would be gutted. Ottawa and Hull would become blackened ruins, with one air-burst bomb dropped over Confederation Square; so would Hamilton, London, Windsor, Kitchener-Waterloo, Copper Cliff-Sudbury, Fort William-Port Arthur, and Chippewa.

Winnipeg would be hit rather harder than any other Canadian city. It lies round and flat. Most of its homes are frame structures. Most of its roofs are cedar shingles. It has the *Continued on page 66*

There IS a defense against the Bomb, claims this writer, and it's time we did something about it

IF ATOMIC WAR COMES....

Inside this circle, a quarter-mile in radius, 90% of the deaths, every building flattened or damaged.

Extreme limit of damage and casualties, two and a half miles from blast.

What an atomic bomb over the corner of Portage and Main could do to Winnipeg. Dead, 40,000; Wounded, 60,000; Homeless, at least 200,000

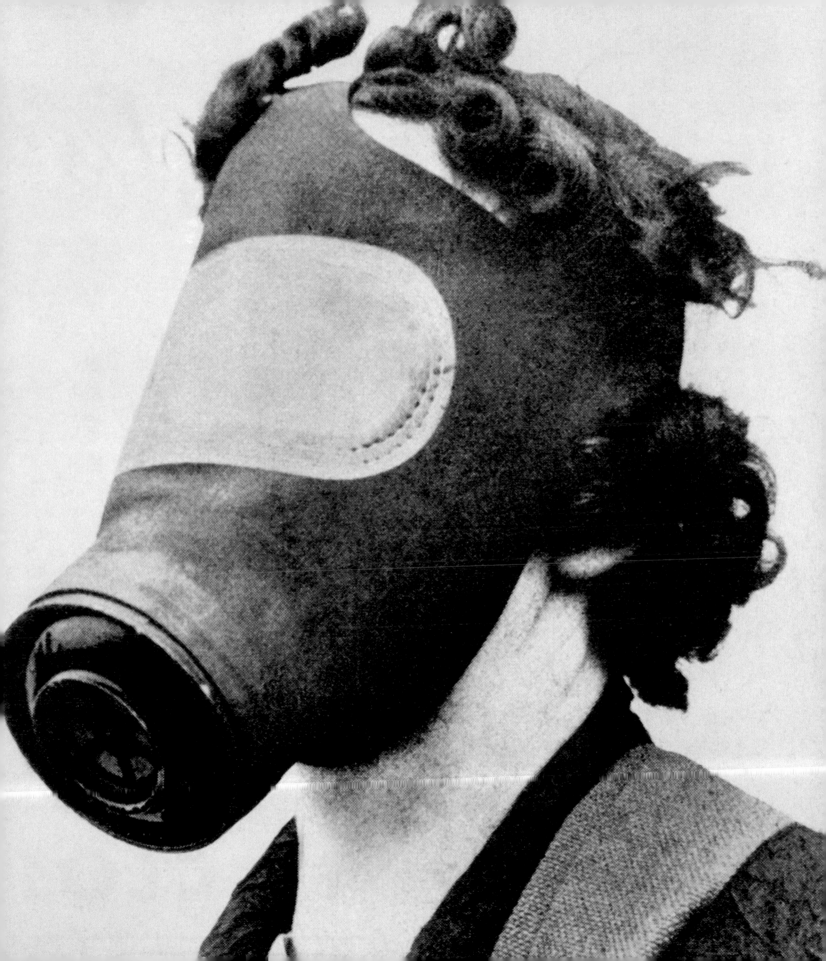

YEAR FOR CRAZY LEGS

Scarborough College, Toronto, provides an appropriately avant-garde background for these sleek, simple clothes. Velour dirndl dress, Poupée Rouge, $45; Burgundy stockings by Phantom; patent-leather shoes by Charles Jourdan, $40; windowpane stocking by Lady Exeter; suede shoe, $38; Yellow cable-stitch Heather Knit from Poupée Rouge, $69; matching handknit knee socks, $15; brown Italian calf shoes, $17.

If you're at university this year and can't afford a Heather knit, try a Mary Quant design for Mary Maxim like the white wool outfit above. If you do-it-yourself from Courtelle Encore yarn, the cost is only $25.30 for size 32 or 34; orange windowpane stocking by Hudson Hosiery from Gambit, Toronto; Italian suede shoes, $55; military coat by Paraphernalia from David II, Toronto, $85; tights by Phantom; Italian calf shoes, $17.

They used to call them gams, and certain women have turned them into twigs, but no matter how you address them, legs turn men on. Especially in the eye-riveting colors available right now. With hemlines all up and down the leg, really great stockings and shoes are necessary. Short skirts are just too bare with plain stockings, so the light bone to Burgundy opaque tones give a sensual, elongated effect without being too naked. Of course, you have to have good legs and well-designed shoes — *nothing* can disguise the ugliness of pointy toes and spike heels no matter what glorious color the legs are sporting. Besides, stockings and co-ordinated shoes are the least expensive way of jazzing up a wardrobe. Switch the shade of stocking and style of shoe and you change the look and feel of a dress.

All shoes are from David's Footwear, Toronto.

FASHION

"YEAR FOR CRAZY LEGS" FASHION SPREAD
November 1967

Opposite page
COVER ILLUSTRATION
November 1913

ADVERTISEMENT FOR REID'S HOLIDAY TOGS
June 15, 1943

They used to call them gams, and certain women have turned them into twigs, but no matter how you address them, legs turn men on. Especially in the eye-riveting colours available right now. . . . Short skirts are just too bare with plain stockings, so the light bone to Burgundy opaque tones give a sensual, elongated effect without being too naked. Of course, you have to have good legs and well-designed shoes—*nothing* can disguise the ugliness of pointy toes and spike heels no matter what glorious colour the legs are sporting.

—"Year for crazy legs," by Marjorie Harris, November 1967

Scarborough and other colleges may not see too many felt hats by Mary Quant ($20), but the yellow and purple dress by Paraphernalia ($45) will go anywhere. Both from David II, Toronto. Yellow stockings by Trimfit; patent-leather sling-back shoes, $25. Black Mary Quant dress from The Establishment, Toronto, $49; caramel stocking by Trimfit; nutmeg rib-on-stripe by Phantom; nailhead patent-leather shoes, $42.

PRODUCED BY MARJORIE HARRIS
PHOTOGRAPHS BY JOHN SEBERT

For a few fearless years in the late 1960s and early '70s, *Maclean's* ran fashion features on a semi-regular basis. Other sample titles from the era: "Go exotic for après-ski" and "It looks as if bathing suits are here to stay, but only just barely."

5

COEXISTENCE

OPENING PAGE FOR THE ARTICLE "BRITISH COLUMBIA'S RACIAL PROBLEM"
Feb. 1, 1930

Opposite page
PASTOR'S DAUGHTER MARIE TSCHETTER (CENTRE) WITH HUTTERITE WOMEN
Fairview, Alta., 1965

We Canadians tend to pride ourselves on residing in an ethnically diverse and tolerant nation, but the blatantly racist views voiced in some *Maclean's* articles from the magazine's early decades tell a different story. By the time Don Newlands photographed Alberta Hutterites in 1965, the views expressed at right in a 1930 article about Asian immigrants were already wildly out of date. But the Hutterites were still subject to discriminatory practices. Under the Communal Property Act, Alberta's pacifist, isolationist Hutterites were one of the religious sects that required special permission to form colonies within 40 miles of each other, and the size of each colony was also restricted. The act was repealed in 1972.

The opinion is general among all classes that something will have to be done sooner or later, and that the longer things are allowed to go on as they are, the worse they will get, and the harder it will be to correct them later. The present trend must be stopped, they say, if white men are to remain the dominant race in this province. . . .

British Columbia wants to remain a white man's country for all time, and in the interest of Canada as a whole it is vitally important that she should.

—"British Columbia's racial problem," by Charles E. Hope, Feb. 1, 1930

6

RECREATIONAL DRUGS

SMIRNOFF AD WITH SINGER ROBERT ("BOB") GOULET
Aug. 13, 1960

Opposite page
"LEN NORRIS GOES TO A NEW YEAR'S PARTY"
Jan. 1, 1951

An inevitable question of the '70s: what should you do if you catch your kid smoking pot? "Be cool," says Milan Korcok at Toronto's Addiction Research Foundation. "Talk to him. Find out how long he has been smoking it and why. Is it curiosity? Does he use it often? You do not pick up the phone and call the police and say, 'I've got a drug addict on my hands.' " Beyond that, unfortunately, even the experts at ARF are stuck for an answer. Well, what should you do if you're at a party and the host is passing around marijuana joints or pills? "Stay with something you know," says Korcok.
—"How to make it to 1979," by Jon Ruddy, January 1970

Over the course of a century, *Maclean's* articles about alcohol and other intoxicants have aired the views of temperance advocates, as well as those with a more relaxed attitude to quaffing or inhaling this or that.

Bob Goulet, Canadian singing star of stage and television

Lunchtime or nightime . . . it's smoother made with Smirnoff

Time is *not* of the essence! The vodka's the thing! And as any good mixer will tell you, Smirnoff is the vodka of vodkas. A martini anybody? A bloody mary? You name it! It's smoother made with Smirnoff.

It leaves you breathless

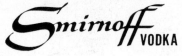
Smirnoff VODKA

HEADLINES

The names still resonate: Vimy Ridge, Dieppe, Suez. Oka and Meech Lake, the Famous Five and the FLQ, the Boyd Gang and the Avro Arrow. You may not remember exactly who or what or where they were, or why they were significant, but you know you *should* know. For these names, once the focus of fleeting headlines, have transcended time and the pages they were printed on. They've become history.

A "fable agreed upon"—that's what Napoleon called history, and he had a point. Like beauty, history is in the eye of the beholder, and what we hand down to future generations are not only the cold facts but the import and emotions we invest in them. Vimy wasn't just a German-controlled ridge in northern France but a place where, at horrendous cost, Canadian foot soldiers helped forge a nation. The Arrow wasn't just a supersonic plane but a reason for national preening—and a still-controversial case of Canadian innovation cut short.

With some news, no passage of time seems required. Pearl Harbor, JFK's assassination and 9/11 all pass the where-were-you-when test: if you were of age, you remember. But even then the historic spin depends on who's doing the telling. For the Americans, Pearl Harbor set off the Second World War; for Canada and its allies, that terrible war was already two years old.

Of course, there's more media now to do the spinning. In the age of the 24-hour all-news channel, repeated reports on the 2003 SARS outbreak spread fears of a global pandemic, while turning Toronto into an international pariah. Imagine the same kind of coverage of, say, the Spanish flu epidemic of 1918-19, which killed more than 20 million people worldwide compared to SARS' global total of fewer than 800. Or take the Salé and Pelletier story from the Salt Lake City Olympics, where the media-stoked uproar over rigged figure skating forced the Games to give the pair gold. You think Canadian women wouldn't have won the vote sooner if Nellie McClung and Emily Murphy had chatted incessantly with some back-in-the-day Peter Mansbridge?

There are potential parlour games aplenty. Who got a giddier response, the cherubic Dionne quints or the charming Pierre Trudeau (or perhaps the cheeky, newly arrived Beatles)? Which city was more chaotic, Winnipeg beset by the bloody strike of 1919 or Montreal traumatized by terrorists in 1970? Who did Canada treat more shamefully, Natives down through the decades or Japanese Canadians in internment times? When were Ottawa's relations with Washington more dismal, during the Vietnam War when Lyndon Johnson thundered to a lecturing Lester Pearson, "You peed on my rug!"—or of late, as Canada scorned America's Iraq entanglement?

Who knows? Discuss. Spin away. There are no right answers, and no end to potential sources of speculation. One hundred years may be an eternity for a magazine, but it's a day trip in the long march of history.

BOB LEVIN (EXECUTIVE EDITOR; JOINED *MACLEAN'S* STAFF IN 1985)

1 2 3 4 5 6 **7 8 9 10 11 12 13 14 15 16 17 18 19 20** 21 22 23 24 25 26 27
54 55 56 57 58 59 60 61 62 63 64 65 66 67 68 69 70 71 72 73 74 75 76

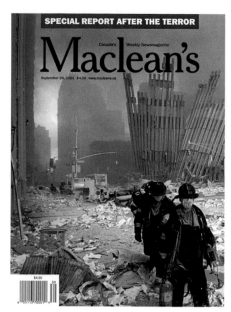

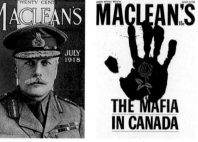

30 31 32 33 34 35 36 37 38 39 40 41 42 43 44 45 46 47 48 49 50 51 52 53
79 80 81 82 83 84 85 86 87 88 89 90 91 92 93 94 95 96 97 98 99 100

7

WEATHER

FUNNEL CLOUD BEHIND A SUBDIVISION
Edmonton, 1987

Opposite page
**OVERFLOWING CHICOUTIMI RIVER DAM
DURING SAGUENAY RIVER SYSTEM FLOOD**
Chicoutimi, Que., 1996

Saguenay River System flooding in 1996 caused 10 deaths; 12,000 residents were driven, boated or airlifted away from swollen rivers and mudslides. When a tornado ripped through Edmonton in 1987, killing 25 people and doing millions of dollars in damage, tennis ball-sized hailstones hit parts of the city that the funnel cloud missed.

The killer winds tore along a five-kilometre-wide path through suburbs and industrial areas on Edmonton's east side. When the storm was over nearly an hour later, houses were destroyed, and cars and trucks had been overturned. An Edmonton policeman told *Maclean's* that the wind's fury blew a dishwasher from Edmonton into a farmer's field at Bon Accord, 30 km away.

The storm toppled steel electrical transmission towers, blew over the cars of a stationary freight train, upended a huge oil-storage tank and flipped a semi-trailer filled with 40 tons of construction equipment onto its roof. Walid Ammar, owner of a restaurant near the trailer park, said: "I could feel the wind spinning. The noise was like a giant vacuum cleaner."

—"A disaster in Edmonton," by John Howse, Aug. 10, 1987

I knew this was the largest police operation in Canadian history. Still I was shocked by the force they used. It didn't take long for a part of the wall to go down. We weren't close enough to see exactly what was going on, but while we were still sussing out the situation the police fired tear gas. Then to our right, we noticed two lines of police moving in. To our left, the police drove two gigantic trucks right through the crowd. There didn't seem to be any way out. Finally, one small street opened up. Out of the zone, everything was eerily quiet. Activists and residents both seemed to be in states of shock and fear.

—Eyewitness account of Sarah Blackstock, a protestor at the Summit of the Americas free trade talks in Quebec City, April 30, 2001

Inflation and postwar unemployment precipitated the Winnipeg general strike of 1919. At the 2001 Summit of the Americas in Quebec City, RCMP officers deployed tear gas, water cannon and rubber bullets, injuring several anti-globalization protestors; the Commission for Public Complaints against the RCMP later described the force used as "excessive."

8

PROTEST

"BLOODY SATURDAY"—AN ANGRY CROWD TOPPLED A CITY STREETCAR
Winnipeg, 1919

Opposite page
PROTESTORS AND POLICE AT THE SUMMIT OF THE AMERICAS
Quebec City, 2001

9

TERROR

THE WORLD TRADE CENTER
New York City, Sept. 11, 2001

We watch, gape-mouthed, wide-eyed as children. We watch because we can't not watch, because if they show it one more time perhaps then we'll believe it.

There have been other American moments like this—TV moments, death caught live, forever with us. Jack Ruby, the assassin's assassin, gunning down Oswald right there in black-and-white. The space shuttle *Challenger*, seven aboard including that smiling, curly-haired teacher, exploding orange, leaving fork-shaped contrails. And now the World Trade Center, soaring icon of financial clout: with the north building already ablaze, cameras record a plane plowing into the south tower, into people's offices, flames shooting unimaginably from the far side; then later the collapse, the once-proud twins succumbing separately, silently (on TV, anyway), an eerie avalanche. We watch, turning to each other in awe, in horror, in that too-human way of the highway rubbernecker: did you see *that?*

We saw it, over and over. Nothing makes it go away.

—"After the terror," by Bob Levin, Sept. 24, 2001

The first regular issue of *Maclean's* to be devoted to a single subject was published after the 9/11 terrorist attacks on the United States.

10

CRISIS

WAR MEASURES ACT INVOKED
Ottawa, 1970

October 1970: When the Front de Libération du Québec (FLQ) kidnapped British trade commissioner James Cross (later freed) and Quebec minister of labour and immigration Pierre Laporte (found murdered Oct. 17), Pierre Trudeau's government took authoritarian action that remains controversial to this day.

After the invocation of the War Measures Act by the federal cabinet at four o'clock in the morning on Fri., Oct. 16, 1970 (but not fully revealed in the house of Commons until 11 a.m.) more than 450 Quebeckers were rounded up by the police, and many dozens more were detained for short periods. . . . All but a handful were released without any charges being laid and, in most cases, only perfunctory interrogations. But the most noticable characteristic of the detainees was their diversity, ranging from Pierre Vallières, the philosopher patron of violent revolution, to university student Les Lascau, who was doing nothing more suspicious than canvassing an apartment building with a public opinion poll for the McGill sociology department when he was arrested.

—"War Measures," from *Rumours of War*, by Ron Haggart and Aubrey Golden, excerpted in *Maclean's* February 1971

Each family group made up a caravan. First came the hayrack, roofed in with canvas, the moving home of the family. Fastened with wire or rope to the sides and ends of the rack were chairs, tables, bedsprings and ends, stable lantern, hay forks and other impedimenta of the farm. The man of the family was driving, and children often peered out from under the canvas hood. Tied behind came the family cow trudging along unprotestingly.

Next came the farm wagon with the high grain box, driven by the wife or a boy or girl, the visible contents a dismantled mower, boxes and bundles of household goods, and, if the owner was lucky, a bag or two of oats. Trailing behind the wagon rattled the buggy in which the children used to drive to school, now surmounted by a crate of hens.

—"The trek to Meadow Lake," by W.J. Mather, April 1, 1932

The photo above dates from 1942, but drought also ravaged the prairies in the early years of the Great Depression. At left, W.J. Mather describes how 10,000 Saskatchewan residents abandoned their failed crops and headed north in 1931, on "the greatest internal migration Canada has seen."

11

DROUGHT

PRAIRIE DUST STORM
Pearce Airport, Alta., 1942

12

TRIUMPH

MARK TEWKSBURY WINS OLYMPIC GOLD
Barcelona, Spain, 1992

Opposite page
**MIKE WEIR AFTER HIS MASTERS WIN,
WITH TIGER WOODS**
Augusta, Georgia, 2003

The Masters isn't just a major champion-ship; it's the most-watched tournament in golf. . . .

The victory immediately propelled him to a level of global stardom that few individual Canadian athletes have known before. Sprinter Donovan Bailey after his 1996 Olympic triumph is perhaps the most recent parallel, but Weir resonates more intimately here because it's golf. Few Canadians have any clue how Bailey achieved what he did, but Canada has the highest per-capita golf participation rate in the world. Millions agonized over every slippery three-foot putt. Last week's "Weir No. 1" headlines were corny, but the sentiment still rang true.
—"So what next, Mike Weir?" by James Deacon, April 28, 2003

Whether the hue is Masters-jacket green or Olympic gold (in the 100-m backstroke, in Mark Tewksbury's case), a moment of athletic triumph is always a colourful experience.

The conditions were such that only those who have endured them can have any adequate conception of what they were. At least knee-deep, some waist deep in a thick, gluey, clayey mud and stagnant, putrid water, they passed the night in the rain. . . . Here and there down that desperate line . . . the angry pop-pop-pop of intermittent rifle-fire, like the windy slamming of many doors, occasionally [gave] way to noisy fusillades as one side or the other became angered at some hit or concentrated their fire on some special movement or the other.

—"At the Front with the Princess Pats," by George Eustace Pearson, April 1915

While serving in France with the Princess Patricia's Canadian Light Infantry— the first Canadian regiment to reach the Front— George Eustace Pearson filed dispatches to *Maclean's*.

13

WW1

CANADIANS RETURNING VICTORIOUS FROM THE BATTLE OF FLERS-COURCELETTE
France, September 1916

Opposite page
IN THE TRENCHES
September 1916

By the time I landed with the first 'rhino' ferry carrying tanks from our ship, wide strips of beach were cleared but the fighting was still violent on the farthest flanks. Carrying only a typewriter I raced up the beach and into Bernières. In the dining room of a small hotel, still miraculously standing, about 300 yards back of the beach, I wrote my first newspaper story. Then I returned to the beach. . . . The scene was a nightmare of exploding mines, dead bodies, mostly German, and live Germans approaching with hands raised high in the air. . . .

A few hours ago I drove to the beach at Bernières to visit the first Canadian military cemetery of the new war in France. In sandy ground, 200 yards from the sea, Canadians who fell in the assault are in neat graves surmounted by flowers brought by local residents.

—"Assault on Normandy," by L.S.B. Shapiro, July 15, 1944

On D-Day—June 6, 1944—*Maclean's* War Correspondent Lionel Shapiro landed with the Third Canadian Division on France's Normandy coast. More than 1,000 Canadians died in the first six days of the Normandy campaign, which initiated the liberation of Europe from Nazi Germany.

14

WW2

MACKENZIE KING, FRANKLIN D. ROOSEVELT AND WINSTON CHURCHILL (FRONT ROW)
Quebec Conference, Quebec City, 1943

Opposite page
CANADIAN TROOPS GOING ASHORE AT BERNIÈRES-SUR-MER ON D-DAY
Normandy, France, 1944

15

CONFLICT

A MOHAWK WARRIOR FACES OFF WITH PRIVATE PATRICK CLOUTIER AT THE KANESATAKE RESERVE
Near Oka, Que., Sept. 1, 1990

Canada's Indian tribes were not conquered like the American Sioux or massacred like the Andean Incas. Yet their lives were—and still are—torn apart by white people who refuse to acknowledge their distinctiveness and their rightful claims to parts of a continent that once was fully their own.

Having spent most of a decade researching and writing the history of the Hudson's Bay Co., which made fortunes for succeeding generations of British investors by trading pots, pans and blankets for valuable furs, I've documented many examples of injustice that took place in those early days. That's ancient history, and it may defy common sense that Canadians in 1990 ought to feel guilty and pay reparations when we had no hand in cheating Indians out of their original land and possessions. But Indians operate on a different calendar; yesterday's insults are only aggravated by the passage of time. They view the present as a prologue for the future; not to act now might snuff out the Indians' flickering hopes of justice ever being done.

—"Haunted by history's lively ghosts," by Peter C. Newman, Aug. 6, 1990

In 1990, the town of Oka, Que.'s decision to expand a municipal golf course precipitated a dramatic confrontation: Mohawks from the nearby Kanesatake reserve argued that part of the land in question was theirs, and set up an armed roadblock to halt the construction. The ensuing standoff between Canadian forces and Mohawk Warriors lasted 78 days, resulted in one police officer's death, and focused attention on unresolved First Nations land claims throughout Canada.

16

EPIDEMICS

SPOT ILLUSTRATION FOR AN ESSAY
Feb. 9, 2004

It struck with devastating suddenness. In Nokomis, Sask., in my own family, my father . . . my mother and the seven of us children were all in bed at the same time. A visiting uncle was also sick. Mother barely managed to prepare meals. Neighbours were no help because they had it, too. Finally the town policeman came to the house to milk the cow and kill a chicken. . . .

An undertaker in Toronto recalls, "At the peak we were holding funerals every hour, day and night. I once went for three days and two nights without sleep. Several times we buried whole families, mother, father and two or three children, within one week. Another undertaker downtown had 23 bodies stacked in a garage for a day because there was no room in his establishment. Double and triple funerals were common."

—"The year of the killer flu," by Max Braithwaite, Feb. 1, 1953

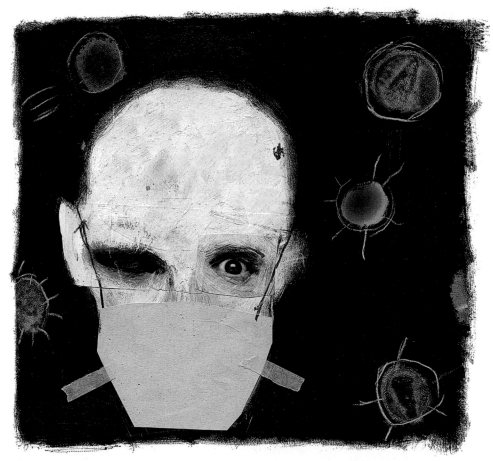

This illustration ran with an essay about how paranoid Torontonians had become about people coughing and sneezing in public, in the wake of the city's 2003 SARS outbreaks. In the end, SARS caused fewer than 50 Canadian deaths, and fewer than 800 worldwide, before its containment. By contrast, the 1918-19 influenza pandemic, or global epidemic, killed more than 20 million people, including 30,000 to 50,000 Canadians. Max Braithwaite survived it, and later wrote about it.

**POLICE SEARCH LEONARD JACKSON'S
APARTMENT AFTER HIS SURRENDER**
Montreal, 1952

Below
**BOYD GANG MEMBER STEVE SUCHAN
WOUNDED IN A POLICE AMBUSH**
Montreal, 1952

In one recent, seven-month period the banks in the Toronto area, which claimed they couldn't afford guards, were robbed of $162,000. But it was the citizens of Toronto who had to foot a bill of more than a million dollars for putting members of the Boyd Gang where they could no longer stick up the banks. This was the cost of arresting, transporting, housing and feeding them; hunting for them after two escapes; providing hospital care for them and the policemen they shot; compensating the family of the officer they killed; stationing police at the banks while they were at liberty.
—"What the Boyd Gang fiasco can teach us," by Allan A. Lamport (Mayor of Toronto), as told to Eric Hutton, Dec. 1, 1952

In 1951-52, several members of the violent, bank-robbing Boyd Gang escaped—at least once, and in some cases twice—from Toronto's Don Jail. Arrested in Montreal in March 1952 after his first jail break, Leonard Jackson took part in another escape six months later. He, William Jackson (no relation) and gang leader Edwin Alonzo Boyd were recaptured near Toronto eight days after the second escape.

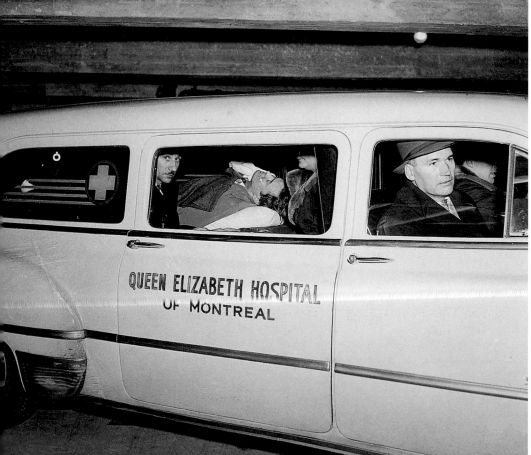

QUEEN ELIZABETH HOSPITAL OF MONTREAL

18

CONTROVERSY

NEWLYWEDS MICHAEL ORR AND THOMAS PATE AT NIAGARA FALLS, ONT.
Maclean's cover photo, March 29, 2004

Opposite page
DAVID PELLETIER AND JAMIE SALÉ SKATE TO (EVENTUAL) OLYMPIC GOLD
Salt Lake City, February 2002

Nebraska won't let them marry—it's in the state constitution—no same-sex unions allowed. So after 11 years as a couple, [Michael Orr and Thomas Pate] . . . drove the 18 hours and 1,500 km from Omaha to Niagara Falls, Ont., . . . to exchange their I dos.
—"Honeymoon heaven," by Danylo Hawaleshka, March 29, 2004

The Russians got five of nine judges' first-place marks even though any modestly informed fan could see that Canadians Jamie Salé and David Pelletier had delivered a technically superior performance.
—"Stuff the silver," by James Deacon, Feb. 25, 2002

The fix was widely thought to be in when Olympic pairs figure skating judges gave 2002 gold to Russia. Canada's silver was later upgraded to a shared gold. In other news, same-sex marital unions remain a divisive issue.

At their peak, flames in the McLure-Barrière and Okanagan Mountain park fires climbed more than 60 m into the forest canopy, and spread at more than 90 m a minute, says [B.C. fire information officer Steve] Bachop. "You can drop all the fire retardant and all the water you've got access to and in most cases it's not going to do anything to slow it down," he says. That latter fire, started on Aug. 16 by lightning, became a "double-headed monster," as one official put it, as winds pushed it north to Kelowna, or south toward the postcard-perfect village of Naramata.

Out of control, by Ken Mac Queen, Sept. 1, 2003

Cumulative drought in Northern Manitoba became so severe in 1989 that bog and wetland areas failed to act as fire-breaks. "They're so dry that fires just whistle across them," fire super-intendent William Medd said at the time. Number of residents evacuated during the province's July 1989 fires: 23,000.

19

FIRE

FIRE AFTERMATH
near Thompson, Man., 1989

Opposite page
**BLAZE RAGING NORTHWARD
TOWARD KELOWNA**
Okanagan Lake, B.C., 2003

20

VICTORY

CELEBRATING VE DAY ON SPARKS STREET
Ottawa, May 8, 1945

This issue of *Maclean's* goes to press as the bells are clanging the peal of Victory and the ink is not dry on the instruments of unconditional surrender which end the Battle of Europe. The air is thick with papers joyously thrown from neighbouring rooftops, and planes are cutting capers in the sky.

We give thanks to those of our nation, those of the Allied Nations, who have fought and suffered and died to make this day a reality.
—"Editorials" page, June 1, 1945

All day long now and into the night we listen to low flying planes which are no longer bent on destruction but are carrying food to Holland and bringing home British prisoners of war. Already in the streets of London one looks at Army lorries or crawling tanks as something incongruous and outdated. Even the uniforms worn by the soldiers seem less military, as if they might transform themselves into civvies at any moment.
—Beverley Baxter's "London Letter,"
June 15, 1945

Sixty years ago, *Maclean's* published twice a month and all magazines had long lead times—hence the time lag in VE Day coverage. Beverley Baxter wrote more than 500 "London Letters" for *Maclean's* between 1935 and 1960.

PASSIONS

Mordecai Richler once described hockey as a "spiritual necessity" in Montreal. He was right about the intensity of the attachment, but wrong about its geographical boundaries. Ask any house leaguer, aging rink rat, hockey mom or puck bunny across Canada and they'll tell you that hockey is this entire nation's greatest passion.

The dream of sipping champagne from Lord Stanley's Cup doesn't end in childhood for Canadians. It's in our blood for life. Much like our passion for the addictive blend of coffee that bears the name of late great Maple Leafs defenceman Tim Horton and is available at a doughnut shop near you.

A cup of joe is certainly a fan favourite among those who enjoy two other long-time Canadian passions—curling and three-down football. That said, so is beer. Nothing goes down smoother at the cottage on a hot summer day than an icy cold Labatt Blue or Molson Canadian—especially with the Tragically Hip or Blue Rodeo pounding from the stereo. (Or maybe you prefer one of Canada's beloved songbirds—from Anne Murray to Avril Lavigne.)

In many ways, our passions have driven us to be better people. Young athletes compete for Olympic gold even though pitiful government support to amateurs makes it nearly impossible to cover the rent. Similarly, passion drives young authors to ignore the meagre earnings from Canadian publishing deals and continue to write great fiction for the love of it. Imagine Canada if Margaret Atwood, Michael Ondaatje or Timothy Findley had decided to make a better living as accountants. The same can be said of the Group of Seven, whose passion for Canada's outdoors led to some of the most inspired art in this country's history.

Some of our passions have brought us closer together as a nation. Where would we be if Pierre Trudeau had lacked the desire to bring home the constitution and create the Charter of Rights and Freedoms in 1981? And let's also remember Terry Fox and Rick Hansen, whose determination gave Canadians a common cause to cheer for. But passions have also nearly torn us apart: the deep-rooted desire for separatism in Quebec has made the prospect of two Canadas a real possibility.

Then there are passions primarily associated with pleasure. Shopping, for instance. Or food. Saskatoon berries, peameal bacon, maple syrup, poutine and beaver tails—Canadians have a rich variety of unique foods to choose from. And of course, we can't forget to talk about sex. Some surveys show that Newfoundlanders like doing it the most, British Columbians do it the least, and Saturday is the most popular day to get it on.

Canadians have a reputation for being understated, but we certainly have a great deal to be passionate about. Consider this: Richler was lured home to Montreal in 1972 by memories of blizzards, hockey, smoked-meat sandwiches and the mountain lakes of his boyhood.

JOHN INTINI (ASSISTANT EDITOR; JOINED *MACLEAN'S* STAFF IN 2000)

1 2 3 4 5 6 7 8 9 10 11 12 13 14 15 16 17 18 19 20 **21 22 23 24 25 26 27**
54 55 56 57 58 59 60 61 62 63 64 65 66 67 68 69 70 71 72 73 74 75 76

21

FLIGHT

**J.A. DOUGLAS McCURDY IN HIS
SILVER DART**
Baddeck, N.S., Feb. 23, 1909

Opposite page
**CF-18 FIGHTERS FLYING IN FORMATION
OVER THE RHINE RIVER**
West Germany, 1987

In 1909, J.A. Douglas McCurdy made Canada's first documented airplane flight—he was airborne for half a mile near Baddeck, N.S. Two years later, poet and *Maclean's* correspondent James P. Haverson described what it was like to be a passenger on an early Toronto flight.

The first thing to indicate we were at last in the air was a curious swaying lurch to the side. It was like the motion of a sailboat slipping over the edge of a wave. It was a boat sailing very close to a very big wind, for we were travelling then at about 40 miles per hour and gaining speed. The wind brought the tears streaming from my eyes. But it brought a pulsing joy into the veins the like of which I have never known.

We lifted, lifted, lifted! We crossed a road about 50 feet up and sailed on over a field. Beside the fence, two men squatted on the ground. I saw their upturned faces and pitied them, for a man in a flying machine is entitled to look down on mere earth crawlers.
—"What it really feels like to be up in the air," by James P. Haverson, October 1911

22

ROMANCE

CROSSING THE THRESHOLD
cover illustration, June 1, 1949

Opposite page
**NEWLYWEDS ROSS THOMAS AND
EILEEN McGREGOR**
cover photo, Toronto, Aug. 12, 2002

Our youth-obsessed society presumes—
or maybe hopes—that the sex drive
disappears after middle age. "Some
people's idea of sex with older people
is, 'Phew—these old people with wrin-
kled bodies, what are they doing,
wanting to be married again, fiddling
around in bed?' " observes Victoria
divorcee Vi Russell, 67. A mention of
seniors and sexuality typically conjures
up Viagra jokes. But while the drug—
and other treatments—have helped
lengthen some seniors' prime time,
there's a greater need to rejuvenate
outmoded cultural attitudes. "The myth
is that if you are over 60, you are a dried-
up old prune and you don't do it," says
[gerontology researcher and author
Lee] Stones. "Of course, you do it."
—"Old flames," by Sharon Doyle Driedger,
Aug. 12, 2002

**Illustrator Oscar Cahén's June bride
was swept off her feet during a postwar housing boom; a 2002 cover story
looked at love among the over-60 set.**

23

SPEED

GÉRARD CÔTÉ OF ST. HYACINTHE, QUE., WINS THE BOSTON MARATHON FOR THE FIRST TIME
Boston, 1940

Opposite page
SPEED SKATER CATRIONA LE MAY DOAN
Calgary, 2002

Profiled in *Maclean's* after his first Boston Marathon triumph in 1940, Gérard Côté also won the event in 1943, 1944 and 1948. Catriona Le May Doan won 500-m Olympic gold at Nagano, Japan in 1998 and at Salt Lake City in 2002. She also won the 1,000-m bronze medal at Nagano.

He's 26 years old, his body is 133 pounds of steel, whalebone, rubber and heart; he's only five feet six inches in height. . . .

That's Gérard Côté, who overnight became the 1940 athletic hero of Canada when, on Patriot's Day, April 19, he raced over the historic Boston marathon course faster than human feet and legs had ever covered that classic race before—26 miles, 385 yards in 2 hours, 28 minutes, 28 ³/₅ seconds.

He earns a few dollars a week in the little city of St. Hyacinthe, near Montreal, as an agent for publications and newspapers; he has no club backing of any kind, his father being his only sponsor; . . . he had 17 dollars in his pocket after travelling from Montreal to Boston by bus.

—"Marathon champ," by Elmer W. Ferguson, June 1, 1940

[I am often asked] "Is there nothing about politics you like?" Of course there is. The spurious indignation when the Prime Minister rises in the Commons to defend the honour and integrity and the bloodlines of the mother of yet another cabinet minister who has to resign three days later is wonderful to behold. The made-for-*The-National* anger of Sheila Copps in Question Period is better than most things you could see on Broadway—and you don't have to pay 75 bucks for a seat. Politics is funnier than sports, and there are more clowns than Eddie Shack. I love it."

"When Politics take when procrastination" by Allan Fotheringham Feb. 12, 1990

Elsewhere in the column quoted at left, Dr. Foth explains that in sports, the major offences are "spearing, tripping, butt-ending, face-mask-grabbing and spitting." In politics, however, "these are minor sins and the main crimes are obfuscation, bafflegab, bluff, procrastination, press releases and public relations officers."

24

POLITICS

ALBERTA PREMIER RALPH KLEIN
Alberta, May 1997

Opposite page
PRIME MINISTER LOUIS ST. LAURENT
location unknown, circa 1950

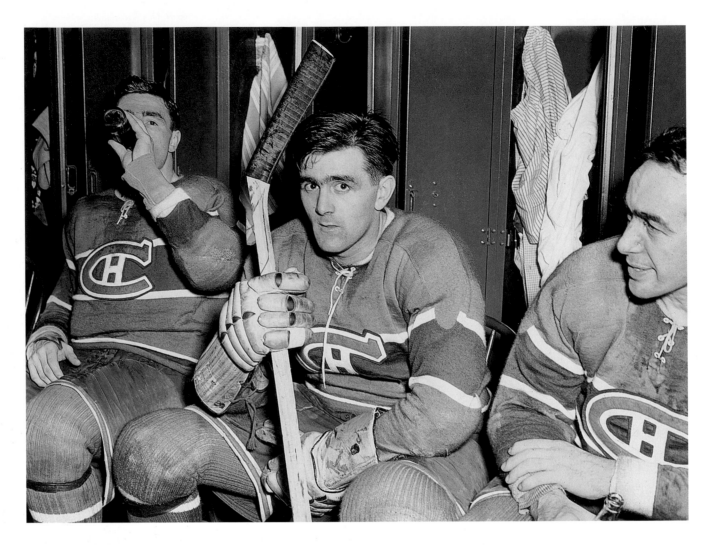

25

HOCKEY

**MAURICE "ROCKET" RICHARD
OF THE MONTREAL CANADIENS**
location unknown, 1950s

Opposite page
**CANADA'S WOMEN'S HOCKEY TEAM
WINS OLYMPIC GOLD**
Salt Lake City, 2002

The 2002 Winter Olympics were doubly golden for Canadian hockey fans. First, the underdog Canadian women's team defeated the United States in the finals. A few days later, the Canadian men's team pulled off the same feat against their U.S. archrivals. For the women, it was the first Olympic gold medal ever; for the men, it was the first in 50 years.

Any moment now Maurice Richard will score the 300th goal of his National Hockey League career and sometime early next spring he will break Nels Stewart's all-time record of 324 goals and thus become the greatest goal scorer in professional hockey history. There is a reasonable likelihood that Richard, who plays for the Montreal Canadiens, will score one or both of these goals while he is lying flat on his back, with at least one non-Canadien hockey player clutching his stick, another hacking at his ankles with a pair of skates and a third plucking thoughtfully at his sweater.

—"Hockey's greatest scoring machine," by Trent Frayne, Nov. 1, 1951

REX WOODS

The cliff-like apartment blocks that girdle [New York City] are rapidly sprouting the new foliage of the TV aerial, and the small talk around town is peppered with tributes to the new gods of the television era: a puppet named "Howdy Doody," a wrestler who calls himself the "Golden Superman" and a none too successful radio comedian named Milton Berle who is currently the hottest thing on the telegriddle.

—"Make way for the one-eyed monster," by Pierre Berton, June 1, 1949

I watched a man wearing a wastepaper basket on his head quarrel with two puppets. I attended a university lecture on anthropology, died with Camille, took one of the most terrible beatings ever experienced by a fight fan, and learned how to make pea soup. I saw some of the most magnificent entertainment I've ever looked at, and a lot of stuff so bad that I blushed for the human race.

—"My first seven days of TV," by Robert Thomas Allen, Jan. 15, 1954

Regular television programming commenced in Canada in September 1952—a few years after the phenomenon had begun taking over U.S. living rooms. But TV demonstrations were a compelling novelty long before most people owned sets: the 1930 photo above was taken in a London studio used for "television recitals."

26

AIRWAVES

TELEVISION STUDIO
London, 1930

Opposite page
AERIAL DILEMMA COVER
ILLUSTRATION BY REX WOODS
July 19, 1958

27

ROLE MODELS

DAVE KEON WITH SOME YOUNG FANS
Toronto, 1963

Opposite page
AVRIL LAVIGNE
Buffalo, N.Y., 2003

Role models don't have to be two-dimensional goody-goodies. In a 1963 *Maclean's* profile of Dave Keon, Peter N. Allison praised the gentlemanly conduct of the Toronto Maple Leafs centre—but described him as "deadly as a rattlesnake with his poke-check."

Lavigne's reluctance to talk shop might be an indication that she *is* overwhelmed by her success, that she's scared to death of a follow-up album, that her career is controlled or manipulated by the record company. But a less cynical view would be that she's just a teenager who's bored of proving herself. "The image out there of me," she says, "is this chick who writes her songs and is herself. And I can see how it could, for some people, look like the label made me up—this chick who wears a tank top and a tie. Whatever, I think the image is way too f---ing pop, it doesn't show my whole realness and my rock, edge side."

It's true that Lavigne likes to rock out more than many of her female contemporaries, but she's a long way from the likes of Courtney Love and Patti Smith. Lavigne's is a parent-friendly, drug-free rock to go along with the musings of what her mother calls a "sensitive" kid.
—"Avril's edge," by Shanda Deziel, Jan. 13, 2003

AISLIN '72.

When I started out to get some facts about the relative merits of horse and automobile for the man with a small country place, I began by asking half a dozen men which they considered cheaper. They all lived in the country and presumably were in a position to know. Without hesitation, and, incidentally without argument, five of them said "horse."

—"The truth about the automobile," by C.O. Morris, reprinted from *Country Life* in *Busy Man's Magazine* (later *Maclean's*), February 1909

Have you ever:
    (a) talked to a Black Panther
    (b) had a Negro as one of your best friends
    (c) voted NDP
    (d) put flower stickers on your car
    (e) quoted Pierre Berton
    (f) been maced

[Answers:] If you've talked to a Black Panther, you've been where the action is; add one point. If you've had a Negro for a best friend, you should know he prefers to be called a black. Lose one point. An NDP vote wins one point. If you spent time putting flowers on your car, you can take them off now and lose five points. To quote Pierre Berton is to lose 10 points—and if you are Pierre Berton, lose 50. For having been maced, you deserve 10 points.

—"How 'now' are you?" quiz by Cathy Wismer, January 1970

Which leader does each of the following statements apply to:

	TRUDEAU %	STANFIELD %	NO COMMENT %
Easiest to believe in	51	42	7
Best informed	65	27	8
Best looking	69	18	13
Best sex partner	67	8	25
Most likely to try marijuana	77	4	19
Dresses in fashion	94	5	1
Most stable in personal life	23	72	5

—results from a *Maclean's*/Goldfarb poll on Canadians' perceptions of PM Pierre Trudeau and Conservative Leader Robert Stanfield, June 1970

Eighteen per cent of adult Canadians say that they have had sex in any type of moving vehicle "such as a car, boat, train, plane or bus." One resident, a 26-year-old male photographer from Shediac, N.B., answered the question by saying "all of the above." Although he later requested anonymity, he told *Maclean's* that he had had intercourse in airplane washrooms, in the back seats of buses and even while driving a car at 100 km/h on the Trans-Canada Highway. His nautical adventures took place in ferryboat washrooms. . . . He added: "Actual intercourse is very awkward while driving. But I tell you, it is exciting."

—"Sex lives of Canadians," by John Barber, featuring findings from a *Maclean's*/Decima poll, Jan. 5, 1987

Generation upon generation of readers have picked up *Maclean's* to find out what percentage of polled individuals felt which way or the other about pretty much everything. The horse-versus-automobile question doesn't get asked much anymore—and if it did the answers would be different—but poll stories about sex and/or politics perennially do well on the newsstand. Multiple-choice questionnaires have also appeared now and then in the pages of *Maclean's*. For the record, only one of them—the 1970 "How 'now' are you?" quiz excerpted at left—ever zeroed in mercilessly on Pierre Berton.

28

POLLS AND QUESTIONNAIRES

CHART FROM "SEX LIVES OF CANADIANS"
Jan. 5, 1987

Opposite page
AISLIN EDITORIAL CARTOON OF PRIME MINISTER PIERRE TRUDEAU AND CONSERVATIVE PARTY LEADER ROBERT STANFIELD
1972

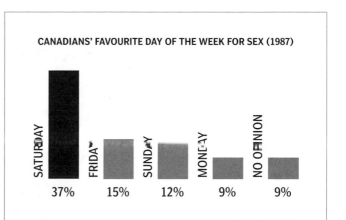

CANADIANS' FAVOURITE DAY OF THE WEEK FOR SEX (1987)

SATURDAY 37% FRIDAY 15% SUNDAY 12% MONDAY 9% NO OPINION 9%

29

CARS

CHRYSLER ADS FOR NEW 1941 MODELS
1940

Opposite page
NISSAN 350Z
Toronto, 2003

It will never be possible to get us out of our cars and into trains and subways, says [motivational researcher Dr. Ernest] Dichter, for the simple reason that most of us subconsciously need the automobile. It is more than a means of transportation: it's an extension of our personalities, the vehicle with which ordinary people are able to feel that they're conquering the world. "By surrounding ourselves with the heavy steel hull of a car, we climb into a womb," says Dichter. "By attaining mastery of its technical instruments, we can use the car to master the elemental world."

—"The car and its prophets," September 1967

The sleek Nissan on the opposite page seems down-to-earth compared to cars forecast nearly half a century ago. A 1958 news item in *Maclean's* mentioned a then-in-development car that would float along "on an air film created by tiny jets streaming through 'levapads' under the vehicle."

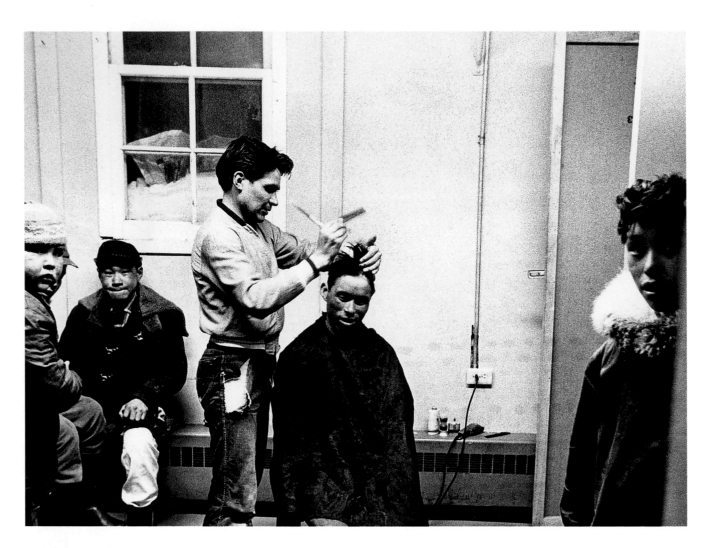

30

TRUST

BARBER AT WORK AT A NORTHERN AFFAIRS OFFICE
east shore of Hudson's Bay, 1961

The excerpt at right is from a profile of Paul Emile ("Red") Tassé, head barber for more than 30 years at Ottawa's Château Laurier hotel. Tassé became an intimate of Mackenzie King and many other prominent politicians—just as barbers and hair stylists everywhere have formed bonds of trust with their regular clientele.

For 30 years now, Mr. King's regular Tuesday afternoon haircut has been the highlight in Tassé's week. So friendly are relations between them that Ottawans out for an evening stroll have more than once come upon the two of them—ex-Prime Minister and Château barber— out for a breath of air together in Major Hill Park. . . .

When King once confided wistfully, "You know, Tassé, I should have been married years ago," Tassé—although an out-and-out family man himself—nevertheless exclaimed, "Oh no, Mr. King. If you'd had a wife you'd never have been Prime Minister all these years. She'd have demanded your time. She'd have involved you in jealousies. There'd have been black sheep among the children. Oh no, Mr. King, no."

—"The man who clipped the King," by Dorothy Sangster, Nov. 1, 1949

We had better make the best of the fact that teenage sex is here to stay and that we adults have been helping to build the kind of society in which it flourishes. . . . [My daughters] are pretty level-headed girls and if, in a moment of madness or by calculated design, they find themselves bedded with a youth (and I trust it will be a bed and not a car seat) I do not really believe the experience will scar their psyche or destroy their future marriages. Indeed I would rather have them indulge in some good, honest, satisfying sex than be condemned to a decade of whimpering frustration brought on by the appalling North American practice called "petting."

—"It's time we stopped hoaxing the kids about sex," by Pierre Berton, May 18, 1963

Pierre Berton joined *Maclean's* staff in 1947 and was managing editor when he left, in 1958. In the early 1960s, he returned briefly as a *Maclean's* columnist—but "Pierre Berton's Page" went on permanent hiatus shortly after he took a progressive stance on teen sex in one of his 1963 columns.

31

SEX

SPOT ILLUSTRATION FOR "THE VIAGRA MYTH"
July 19, 2004

32

FOOD

**SNOWSHOE CLUB MEMBERS EATING
AN OUTDOOR MEAL OF BEANS**
near Montreal, 1956

Opposite page
**CHEF MICHAEL STADTLÄNDER (RIGHT)
IN HIS EIGENSINN FARM KITCHEN**
near Collingwood, Ont., 2003

The six-course dinner . . . includes
an unforgettable soup of lobster . . .
periwinkles and white asparagus, then
squab (pigeon) and foie gras with a
potent, marjoram-infused reduction,
sweet Georgian Bay pickerel accompanied by wild leeks and a vibrant medley
of pepper cress, sorrel and chives,
and a rhubarb meringue hazelnut tart.
—"Tastes of the true north," by Patricia
Hluchy, July 1, 2003

National culinary sophistication evolved
considerably between 1956, when
Maclean's devoted several thousand
words to "How Beans Built Canada,"
and Patricia Hluchy's 2003 visit to
Eigensinn Farm, where master chef
Michael Stadtländer prepares state-
of-the-art Canuck cuisine.

33

SHOPPING

HUDSON'S BAY COMPANY STORE
location unknown, circa 1950

Opposite page
COVER ILLUSTRATION BY A.J. CASSON
Dec. 1, 1935

The 1935 cover illustration at right depicts a more urban scene than is generally associated with the Group of Seven, but it is in fact an A.J. Casson. He started out as a commercial artist and continued to take on illustration assignments long after becoming a member of the Group in 1926.

All right, watch yourself. Stick to the outer fringe of counters. Remember what happened last Christmas when you sailed blithely into Sampson's Department Store. Got sucked into that terrible rip tide near Ladies' Hosiery. Rammed by a notion-going liner. Beached, gasping and helpless, over the umbrella counter. Then you lost your head and bought three umbrellas. Who did you know that could use an umbrella? Answer: nobody. This year let's have less of that. . . .

Now, where's that shopping list? Ah, here we are:

Uncle Fred............tie ($1.50)	Aunt Bertha.....tie ($ .75)
Brother John........tie ($1.50)	Wife.....................? ($5.00)
Cousin Willie........tie ($1.50)	

Let's see, where are the ties?

—"Shopping is such sweet sorrow," by Eric Nicol, Dec. 15, 1948

34

SPACE

**ROBERTA BONDAR AND OTHER *DISCOVERY*
CREW MEMBERS BEFORE THEIR MISSION**
Cape Canaveral, Florida, 1992

Opposite page
**FIRST DEPLOYMENT OF THE *COLUMBIA*
SPACE SHUTTLE'S CANADARM IN SPACE**
1981

In January 1992, *Discovery* crew member Roberta Bondar became the second Canadian astronaut and the first Canadian woman to travel in space. She told *Maclean's* that her scientific career began 35 years earlier, with research on tent caterpillars—she kept them in the fridge of her family's Sault Ste. Marie, Ont. home.

My crewmates joked, "We're going over Canada—boring. It's snowbound and inhospitable." But the snow brought out the beauty. It gave it different dimensions. The rivers were clearer because of the ice. The first time we passed over, I was playing a tape of O Canada sung by a policeman in the Soo. It was a pre-sleep time and I had the earphones on. It was marvellous—better than watching someone at the Olympics get the gold medal and see the flag go up.

—"A report from space," by Roberta Bondar (in conversation with Hilary Mackenzie), Feb. 24, 1992

35

SPORTS (OTHER THAN HOCKEY)

SKIING AND DOGSLEDDING AT GROUSE MOUNTAIN
Vancouver, 1930

Peter Gzowski was managing editor of *Maclean's* when he wrote about learning to ski. Years later he held the top job of editor at the magazine— very briefly, in 1970— before becoming one of Canada's most popular broadcasters.

Some resorts in eastern Canada are . . . guaranteeing they can teach you to ski in a week—though they are not explicit about how well. Last spring, I set out to see how well one resort's instructors could do with me. . . .

Did I learn to ski? Well, yes, I guess. I'm certainly not going into any races for a while, but I will be doing some more skiing. I learned enough, in other words, to be infatuated, if not enough to do standing jumps. Falling, scrambling and probably looking for all the world like a praying mantis on boards, I had the time of my life. I got suntanned, slimmer, a little bruised and a lot happier. If the purpose of ski weeks is to teach you to *want* to ski, then I am here to report their success.

—"How I nearly learned to ski in a week," by Peter Gzowski, Dec. 15, 1962

Soon we were in a region of hill, forest, lake and river, cooled by the reliable refrigerating apparatus of [Lake] Huron and perfectly designed for the camper, fisherman and painter. I began to understand why the Group of Seven had gone gently mad in these surroundings. Their gaudy brush strokes seem extravagant only to those who have not beheld the artists' model.

—"Northern Ontario," by Bruce Hutchison, March 17, 1956 (part of the series "Bruce Hutchison rediscovers the unknown country")

In his "unknown country" series, Bruce Hutchison noted that the air at twilight near Cobalt, Ont., carried a scent of wild rose, spruce, muskeg and balm of Gilead. To him, it was "a smell sweet with boyhood memory and a man's valedictories."

36

THE LAND

A SEPTEMBER GALE, GEORGIAN BAY
BY ARTHUR LISMER
1920

37

ICONS

STANLEY CUP CELEBRATIONS
Edmonton, 1980s

Opposite page
ANNE MURRAY BACKSTAGE AFTER A CONCERT AT HAMILTON PLACE
Hamilton, 1974

We've always seen her as she was when she burst onto the scene some five years ago, with a don't-care attitude and a fawn-like shyness. She was a mail-order package from the Maritimes and she arrived just when Canada was turning on to its own worth. . . . In some ways, she became part of the Canadian nationalism movement. . . .

[Anne Murray's] most important consideration right now is to make it very, very big in the United States. And if that means giving up her image as queen of the high-school prom, that's just part of the price she has to pay.

—"The flip side of Anne Murray," by Larry LeBlanc, November 1974

In 1974, Larry LeBlanc interviewed and photographed Anne Murray at a pivotal point in her career; approximately a decade later, Steve Simon photographed hockey's holy grail in a less-than-wholesome setting.

THE COUNTRY

Where do you start when discussing Canada, the land? Well, it's a big country; and it's almost alone at the top of the world with its eccentricities, something for which the rest of the world should be profoundly grateful.

The conventional shorthand is that we have too much geography and not enough history. We say this as though it were a problem. In reality, most countries have too much history. Most of their history is about other people taking away bits of geography. We have all this geography because so few people have ever committed history against us. Yes, yes: assorted Europeans did come here and commited history against the First Nations, but since then it's been pretty quiet.

Once I was served up as the local expert for lunch with a delegation of visiting Belgian journalists. I offered piquant anecdotes about our malfunctioning federation, our rapacious neighbour, our mix-and-match ethnic mosaic, our kleptophilic leaders. Eventually one of the Belgians put his fork down, leaned forward and regarded me as you might regard a rich cousin complaining about a hangnail. "You understand that we dream about Canada, don't you?"

Oh. Right. Sorry. If you watch the old newsreel footage of Pierre Trudeau telling some swell Yankee audience that Canada's life is like a mouse's sleeping next to an elephant, what's striking is how much more laughter and applause he expects than what he gets from the line. Many other countries could only hope to be a mouse next to an elephant. I was in Poland a few months ago. They've spent eternity, basically, between two lions—Russia and Germany—and, at intervals, they get eaten. Poles are amazed to learn that Canadians consider themselves the world's foremost authority on the topic of unruly neighbours.

So we are untroubled, comparatively speaking, as we contemplate the long horizons and the long nights. All this study time, oddly, has not done wonders for the national attention span. History is not our strong suit, which is OK because at least it allows us to find novelty in some pretty stale story lines. There are nationalists in Quebec! The fish are running out on the Atlantic coast! Toronto keeps making money! Damnedest thing.

One reason for the failure, as television, of the CBC's "Greatest Canadian" search is that Canada's heroes have risen to challenges many people in the world would see as blessings. Our statesmen struggle to hold together a country very few would ever want to leave, except maybe out of boredom. They struggle to protect us against a neighbour of—there is no polite way to say this—conspicuous benevolence. Our soldiers have to travel a long way to pick fights. Our artists struggle with prosperity and ample workspace. Never mind history or geography: the commodity in shortest supply around here is the sympathy of strangers. We have to manufacture our own supply at home. It's a tough job but we have always been up to it.

PAUL WELLS (BACK PAGE COLUMNIST; JOINED *MACLEAN'S* STAFF IN 2003)

1 2 3 4 5 6 7 8 9 10 11 12 13 14 15 16 17 18 19 20 21 22 23 24 25 26 27
54 55 56 57 58 59 60 61 62 63 64 65 66 67 68 69 70 71 72 73 74 75 76

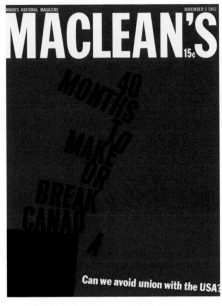

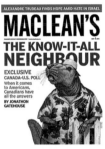

38

MOUNTIES

UNKNOWN MOUNTIE
location unknown, circa 1920

Opposite page
**PRIME MINISTER MACKENZIE KING GREETS
QUEEN ELIZABETH ON PARLIAMENT HILL**
Ottawa, 1939

The Mountie adapts his clothing to the particular brand of climate he has to face in his outdoor work. But the type of man in the clothing is pretty much the same from ocean to ocean—six feet in his sock-feet, or pretty close to it, clean-limbed and clear-eyed. He is taught to be tolerant and to use firearms only as a last resource. It is only in the motion pictures that the Mounties nowadays use up much ammunition. Their chief pride is in landing a prisoner in a man's fight— if there has to be a fight.
—caption for "Real days of derring do," a *Maclean's* excerpt from R.G. MacBeth's book *Policing the Plains,* December 1921

Author R. G. MacBeth served with the Winnipeg light infantry in the 1880s and later became a Winnipeg pastor.

As [Trudeau] sat down with the Queen to sign the proclamation at 11:35 a.m. (EST) Saturday, the first drops of an eventual downpour spattered the hand-lettered parchment crafted from Manitoba flax. Errant droplets smudged the queen's red-lettered introductory protocol greeting and the black Mont Blanc ink signature of [registrar general] André Ouellet. . . . Instead of a quick trip to the printer and distribution across the nation, the proclamation was dried out during the weekend under the watchful eye of calligrapher John Whitehead.

—"Rebirth of a nation," by Robert Lewis, April 26, 1982

For 51 years, Canadian politicians lobbied for patriation of the Canadian Constitution from Britain. On April 17, 1982, Canada acquired a constitution that was, as the Queen phrased it, "truly Canadian at last." Rex Woods painted *Flag Debate* for a 1954 *Maclean's* cover; Canada officially raised its own flag for the first time on Feb. 15, 1965.

39

NATIONHOOD

PIERRE TRUDEAU AND QUEEN ELIZABETH AT THE PATRIATION CEREMONY
Ottawa, April 17, 1982

Opposite page
DETAIL FROM "FLAG DEBATE" COVER ILLUSTRATION
July 1, 1954

40

GREAT ONES

**WAYNE GRETZKY TOPS GORDIE HOWE'S
ALL-TIME POINTS RECORD**
Edmonton, 1990

Opposite page
**MINNIE SHAW WITH RED WINGS PLAYERS
RESIDING AT HER BOARDING HOUSE
(LEFT TO RIGHT: MARTY PAVELICH, RED
KELLY, METRO PRYSTAI AND GORDIE HOWE)**
Detroit, circa 1951

[As at] most birthday parties for 18-year-olds, cameras clicked and at least one of the envelopes held money. But Wayne Gretzky's party last year was held at centre ice at the Edmonton Coliseum, the pictures were for newspapers, and the envelope held $5 million.

Before he had tasted his first legal drink, the once and future "Great Gretzky" had signed his second million-dollar-plus contract to ply his trade. . . .

There's another fellow who was tagged for greatness at 18. He didn't get quite the same initial reception, but then again the Second World War had just recently ended, there were just six teams in the NHL and million-dollar salaries sounded Orwellian. After a year in the hockey backwater of Omaha, Nebraska, the kid from Floral, Saskatchewan, Gordie Howe, made it in the big leagues.

—"The kid that could, and the man who has," by Hal Quinn, Feb. 11, 1980

41

THE NORTH

AFTER THE GOOSE HUNT
Lake Mistassini, Que., 1995

Opposite page
ARCTIC HUNTER WITH MUSKOX HORN BOW AND ARROW
Bathurst Inlet, Northwest Territories (now Nunavut), 1949

The image at right dates from 1949. Five years later, Pierre Berton—*Maclean's* managing editor at the time—wrote about his own travels through Canada's Far North. In 1995, *Maclean's* profiled Matthew Coon Come, grand chief of the Grand Council of the Cree of Quebec. The image above did not run with the article, but others from the same shoot did.

There is a saying in the north that after five years in the country every man is an expert, after 10 years a novice. I was born and raised in the north. I've worked in a Klondike gold camp, travelled the Yukon and Mackenzie by boat, driven up the Alaska Highway, ridden an Eskimo sled on Baffin Island, eaten buffalo at Fort Smith, reindeer at Aklavik and moose at Whitehorse, watched gold bricks poured at Dawson, uranium milled at Great Bear and pitchblende staked south of Yellowknife. This summer, to gather material for this article, I've already travelled 15,000 miles, with more thousands ahead of me. Yet to me, as to most northerners, this land is still an unknown quantity.
—"The mysterious north," by Pierre Berton, Nov. 15, 1954

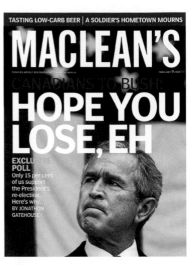

TASTING LOW-CARB BEER | A SOLDIER'S HOMETOWN MOURNS

MACLEAN'S

CANADIANS TO BUSH:

HOPE YOU LOSE, EH

EXCLUSIVE POLL
Only 15 per cent
of us support
the President's
re-election.
Here's why.
BY JONATHON
GATEHOUSE

MACLEAN'S 15¢

ca 1960 ★ a 100-page report on the people all the shouting is abou

BEST ISN'T GOOD ENOUGH: A SEARCH FOR AMERICAN EXCELLENC

E THE AMERICAN NEGRO STANDS IN THE BROWN MAN'S WORL

NZIE PORTED ON TAPS: THE TRUTH ON THE FACE OF THE USA

Incredible women of Madison Avenue--what it costs to out-man me

D TOYNBEE ON THE AMERICAN CHARACTER ★ *Barbara Moon on her worship*

ROVERE ON AMERICA'S SMUG NORTHERN NEIGHBOR ★ *Peter C. Newman on Wall Stree*

a color collection of an unexpected America that has almost eluded time

According to the unnamed "American" excerpted on the opposite page, the average Canadian "asks the Lord each night and morning" to make him responsible, and thinks: "The government should be responsible, the courts should be responsible, the newspapers should be responsible, the beverage rooms should be responsible, teachers and children and hockey players and radio comedians—everybody should be responsible."

"*You're conservative and reticent,*

"*Canadians seem to be happier than Americans*

"*Canadian businessmen want the same money*

"*Canadian union men are less aggressive, lower*

These are among the views of more than a hundred different Americans who know Canada — some well, some only fleetingly. They are nobody's official opinion, but they, and others like them, offer perhaps the clearest picture yet of

WHAT AMERICAN

BY SHIRLEY MAIR

WHILE CANADA AND THE U.S. were worrying publicly early this winter about their official relations, I set out to find out about another kind of relationship between peoples. Over the course of a few weeks I interviewed more than a hundred Americans who had come to Canada *unofficially*, to work, to live or just to visit. I asked them to tell me frankly what they thought of Canada and Canadians. I promised them first that I would use none of their names, and in the report that follows I have even scrambled some identities so that no one will be able to guess who's talking.

As far as it's possible to tell, I got the frank and honest answers I was seeking. One manufacturing agent, who makes frequent trips to Canada, said: "If you're going to quote me by

name, my opinion of Canadians is that they're a great, industrious, intelligent people. But if you don't use my name, I'll tell you that I really think they're smug, lazy, carping bores."

Not many opinions were as brutal as that. Not many, in fact, were hostile at all. Few of the Americans I talked to seemed to be *eager* to criticize Canada, but almost no one backed down from the opportunity to speak bluntly. I found that many Americans like us for virtues we aren't usually aware of — just as, of course, some Americans *dislike* us for defects we don't usually admit we have.

Almost invariably, the Americans started by saying there was no difference between the two countries. And then they'd move on to enumerate (sometimes for more than an hour and a half) all the disparities.

More than any other group of foreigners in

Canada, Americans seem to assimilate quic almost painlessly. One Texan who arrived c a couple of months ago said proudly. " aren't going to believe this but the first w I arrived I managed to wangle a ticket t Canadien-Leaf game." A man from Ariz was willing to forgive a lot because Car had introduced him to curling. He added: " summer the wife and I are going to drive Trans-Canada for two weeks. A Cana buddy of mine says the restaurants along way are pretty bad. I told him, 'Look, you've never eaten on Route 66.' "

While the Americans here have a nat curiosity and often want to "go native," also tend to make snap judgments without ing all the facts. The result is often a mishr of irritating errors. "I told my friends home," an executive from Vermont said. "

22

MACL

CANADA/U.S. RELATIONS

OPENING SPREAD FOR "WHAT AMERICANS REALLY THINK ABOUT US"
April 20, 1963

Opposite page
COVERS
Feb. 9, 2004 (top); Nov. 5, 1960

you're blunt. No one is as honest as a Canadian"

st they are more contented and more balanced"

rican executives, but they won't work as hard"

more patient and more persevering"

ALLY THINK ABOUT US

adians didn't like their Senate, they
vote the same guys in next time."
ss the Americans are, perhaps, more
open-handed in their dealings with
than any other nation. And they
showing their ignorance — some-
don't even mind appearing rude.
either.
the time I was talking privately to
at least two visitors treated Canada
ghly in public. David Susskind, a
television producer and performer,
adian TV that, among other things:
men are the most sublimely dull on
the earth . . . They don't laugh as
mericans because their juices are all
Shortly after, Jim Murray, a Los
mes columnist, flew to Edmonton to
ockey game between the Edmonton

Flyers and the Los Angeles Blades. He wrote:
"Edmonton is a nice town. I think they bought
it at Sears Roebuck and assembled it here.
They should have left it in the box."
    And crass ignorance, publicly or privately
displayed, is, of course, not rare. Nine years
ago, the U. S. Chamber of Commerce published a booklet called *Are Canadians Really?*
Many of the points it raises still apply. The
editor of *Are Canadians Really?*, S a m u e l
Ericsson, says in an introduction that the booklet's purpose was to give basic information and
clear up misconceptions about Canada. Much
of it is pretty basic, all right. "The prime
minister is the real boss man of Canada," it
says at one point. At others, it carefully explains that Canadians don't live in igloos or
hibernate; Canadian school children are taught
to be literate at the same age as American chil-

dren, and Canada is not owned by Britain. But
Ericsson has some shrewd observations to
make about Canadians and Americans who do
know each other. "It's a popular notion," he
writes, "that Canadians and Americans beam
so warmly at each other across their boundary
line that the Great Lakes never quite freeze
solid. The truth is that these smiles sometimes
resemble the twitchings of the lips that result
from gas pains."
    Only a few of the Americans I talked to
waxed as violently anti-Canadian as the manufacturing agent or as Susskind and Murray, but
none of them were unqualified in their praise
of Canada. Not surprisingly, perhaps, most of
the Americans who know Canada said they
liked it. The longer they stay, it seems, the
stronger the affection becomes. Many com-
plained to me CONTINUED ON PAGE 51

This past year Americans decided to demonize Canadians. That's pretty obvious. Apparently we harbour terrorists, our writers who get nominated for the Booker Prize aren't even Canadians— they just collect their mail here—and worst of all, we use metric.

Most of us can remember the exact moment when we realized the Americans don't like us any more. It was during the post-9/11 Bush address to Congress when he stopped to thank America's very best friend in the entire universe . . . England. Huh? And then their next best friend, Mexico, and then somewhere between Cameroon and Cape Verde came Canada. A few years ago even, our national feelings would have been stung by such a slight. But recently? So what.
—"Strong and free," by Douglas Coupland, Nov. 25, 2002

There may be a Canadian somewhere who doesn't know all about the U.S.A., and who isn't prepared to enumerate 11 major improvements urgently needed south of the border, but such a Canadian I have yet to meet.
—"The Canada I see," by An American, May 1, 1946

From the front seat of a white United Nations jeep, Maj. Peter Devlin has witnessed firsthand the destruction of war. Despite 14 years' service with the Canadian Forces, the 32-year-old officer from London, Ont., admits surprise at the wide-scale damage that he has observed on daily reconnaissance missions in Croatia, where he is part of an international peacekeeping force. "Some of the small villages have been completely levelled," he told *Maclean's* last week. "There are very few houses in the rural areas that have roofs or glass left, and the belongings of many homes have been scattered."

—"Stepping into the fray," by Hilary Mackenzie, April 20, 1992

The Canadian Forces' role in the Second World War liberation of the Netherlands and the supply of postwar aid cemented strong ties between the nations. Part of a 1990s United Nations peacekeeping force in the former Yugoslavia, Canadian soldiers attempted to restore order in a chaotic time of factional violence and redrawn borders.

43

CANADIANS OVERSEAS

CANADIAN PEACEKEEPERS AMID RUINS
Croatia, 1993

Opposite page
TROOPER N. RUSSEL OF THE FORT GARRY HORSE PRESENTS TOYS TO DUTCH BOY
Doetinchem, the Netherlands, 1945

44

NEWCOMERS

**IMMIGRANT WORKERS AT THE PEERLESS
CLOTHING COMPANY**
Montreal, 1992

Opposite page
BRITISH IMMIGRANTS ARRIVING AT PIER 21
Halifax, circa 1930

In its early decades, *Maclean's* ran some immigration stories that now make for repellent reading—stories with headlines such as "Shall we bar the yellow race?" (May 15, 1922). Prejudice hasn't magically disappeared since then, but Canada has become proudly and profoundly multicultural.

Five years ago Vietnamese-born Thien Chi Tran's home was . . . a refugee camp in Thailand. Now, he plays second violin in the Calgary Civic Symphony. He fishes and camps, and this fall Thien, 30, began a qualifying year at the University of Calgary. He became a Canadian citizen in June, and this summer he married Sandra Taylor, a teacher specializing in English as a second language. "The first time I felt I belonged here," he recalled, "is when Calgary made the Stanley Cup finals."
—"Opening the doors," by Ken MacQueen, Oct. 13, 1986

45

STATESMEN

SIR WILFRID LAURIER, PRIME MINISTER FROM 1896 TO 1911
location unknown, circa 1910

Opposite page
PIERRE TRUDEAU EXECUTES A PROTOCOL-DEFYING PIROUETTE BEHIND THE QUEEN'S BACK AT BUCKINGHAM PALACE
London, 1977

[There is a Laurier whom] not many people see outside of deputations and axe-grinders—Laurier in his private office in the Eastern Block. . . . This is not the wary politician up to every move in a game full of sharp corners; this is not the spellbinder nor the sunny smiler; this is not even the practical statesman. This is a reserved and god-like being—Jove in a morning coat—seated high above our judgments. What his air conveys more than any-thing else is a profound detachment from the sordid details. He does not fit into the devious game of policies as lesser men play it. He will not stain his mind by looking at their tricks and subterfuges. This is Laurier sitting for his picture in the gallery of fame. He must bear himself as if he already belonged to history.
—"The four Lauriers," by H. Franklin Gadsby, October 1911

46

WINTER

ICE STORM CRIPPLES THE EAST
Montreal, January 1998

Opposite page
**RESERVE SOLDIERS DIGGING OUT TORONTO
AFTER RECORD SNOWFALL**
Toronto, January 1999

In Montreal, an eerie calm hung over the downtown area as almost all stores and businesses shut down. . . . Major hospitals lost their primary power, traffic lights failed, the Metro (subway system) was closed, radio and television stations lost their broadcast signals, and some grocery stores reported panic buying of supplies— even as banks closed and banking machines short-circuited, depriving many people of the money needed to buy goods. . . . As Canadian Forces personnel moved into affected areas to offer help, they found pitch-black, silent streets, makeshift rescue centres and soup kitchens, and devastated landscapes littered with ruined automobiles and homes.
—"Ice age," by Anthony Wilson-Smith, Jan. 19, 1998

The ice storm of January 1998 caused extensive damage and power outages in Quebec and eastern Canada; a year later Toronto took a lot of ribbing from the rest of the country when Mayor Mel Lastman called in the army to dig out the city after a record snowfall.

47

CASTOR CANADENSIS

**DIANA, PRINCESS OF WALES, MEETS
NEEDJEE THE BEAVER AT SCIENCE NORTH
AS ONTARIO PREMIER BOB RAE (LEFT) AND
PRINCE CHARLES LOOK ON**
Sudbury, Ont., 1991

What a fortunate fluke of history it was that the fur trade played such an important role in Canada's early economy. The beaver, as Mary Lowrey Ross argues in the 1944 article at right, is the perfect embodiment of all traits Canadian.

The beaver is a sensible animal with strong domestic instincts. He doesn't leap about like the kangaroo or cavort like Chantecler. He doesn't scream like the eagle or roar like the lion. He's just everlastingly practical and constructive. Leave him alone to cut down trees, slap up a batch of mud for cement and build a nice natural environment for his little ones and he's perfectly happy. He hasn't any time for nonsense.

Canadians have no time for nonsense either. We work hard, live sensibly and try as far as possible to keep from making ourselves ridiculous.

—"We are not funny," by Mary Lowrey Ross, July 1, 1944

48

ACCOUNTABILITY

MAN CONTEMPLATING BARNETT NEWMAN'S *VOICE OF FIRE*, NATIONAL GALLERY OF CANADA
Ottawa, 1990

Can the National Gallery of Canada assure us taxpayers that the controversial painting *Voice of Fire* is not hanging upside down?
—"Letters" page comment from Harry Allen of Victoria, April 9, 1990

In 1990, National Gallery curators found themselves in the hotseat after spending $1.76 million—nearly two-thirds of the institution's annual acquistions budget at the time—on *Voice of Fire*, a 1967 painting by U.S. Abstract Expressionist Barnett Newman. Miraculously, the controversy died down before government officials could appoint a Royal Commission.

49

RESOURCES

HIBERNIA OIL FIELD PLATFORM WELL IN THE JEANNE D'ARC BASIN, 315 KM EAST OF ST. JOHN'S, NFLD.
1988

Opposite page
CLEAR-CUTTING IN B.C.'S FOREST
1998

At right, stumps—burned to promote regeneration—scar a clear-cut section of B.C. forest. Above, the economy-versus-ecology debate also rages on the east coast, where platform wells access the Hibernia oil field, underlying part of the Grand Banks.

The place is called Clayoquot Sound—pronounced CLACK-wit—an area of fjords and fog-shrouded mountains and temperate rain forest boasting trees more than 1,000 years old and 250 feet tall. They are breathtaking in their beauty, considerable in their commercial value. Tree-huggers want to save them, fearing the devastation of a precious resource. Tree-cutters want to harvest them, fearing for their jobs. . . .

Who's the bad guy in this story? The environmentalists? The main logging company, Vancouver-based MacMillan Bloedel? The B.C. Government that, last April, decided to allow logging in two-thirds of Clayoquot's old-growth forest while preserving the rest—a Solomonic split that satisfied no one?

It all depends on who's telling the tale.

—"A forest fable," by Bob Levin, Aug. 16, 1993

The enthusiastic, forgiving cheers that greeted Lévesque in a Montreal arena after the results were out proved that Quebec nationalism remains a Damoclean force hanging over the constitutional conference table. Tearfully, the premier left the stage with a sad wave and a promise of another referendum rendezvous: "Till next time."

Just moments later in another, calmer arena, [Quebec Liberal Party leader Claude] Ryan rubbed his hands in glee, consulted his journalist's notebook and warned the rest of the country: "Our fellow Quebeckers will ask us to be firm in the defence of their interests." In Ottawa, Prime Minister Pierre Trudeau said his joy was tempered by thoughts of the disappointment of 'yes' supporters: "We have all lost a little in this referendum."

—" 'Non'—what now?" by David Thomas, May 26, 1980

It took 128 years to make Canada into the country that it is today—and 10 hours of voting and a margin of only 53,498 votes to almost break with that past and reshape both the map and the country's future. No, 50.6 per cent, total votes: 2,361,526. Yes, 49.4 per cent, 2,308,028 votes. In however much time remains to Canada as a united country, those figures are likely to stay burned on the consciousness of federalists and Quebec sovereigntists alike. By that narrowest of margins, the dream of preserving one existing nation almost died on Monday night, and the dream of building a new, smaller one within Quebec was thwarted—for now.

—"A house divided," by Anthony Wilson-Smith, Nov. 6, 1995

I am a 63-year-old Québécois, part of the silent majority. I would like to express my frustration at having been led to vote No. I wanted to vote Yes because I am very unhappy with the way Quebec has been treated by English Canada. I wanted to vote Yes because I believe that 80 per cent of English-Canadians hate the fact that bilingualism was forced upon them because of Quebec. I wanted to vote Yes because I know that bilingualism does not work. And I wanted to vote Yes because I do not believe one-third of what the politicians for the No side told me. Yes, my heart told me to vote Yes. But I said to myself, is it right to let only my emotions guide me in making such an important decision? I voted No because I do not believe one-third of what the politicians for the Yes side told me. There were too many unanswered questions. You probably think that common sense and logic won over sentiment. You are wrong. The main reason I voted No is that I am a coward.

—"Letters" page comment from Jean-Claude Salman of Anjou, Que., Nov. 13, 1995

The question of whether Quebec should remain a Canadian province, become an entirely separate entity or pursue the middle ground of sovereignty association is probably the most divisive issue in all of Canadian history. When Parti Québécois leader René Lévesque held the first Québec referendum on May 20, 1980, approximately 60 per cent of the Quebec electorate chose the status quo over a mandate to pursue sovereignty association with the rest of Canada. In a second referendum, held on October 30, 1995, Quebec once again said no to sovereignty—but only by the narrowest of margins. Separatism in this country has never been simply a Francophone-versus-Anglophone affair; as Jean-Claude Salman's letter to the editor indicates, it's all too possible for an individual to hold Yes and No views simultaneously.

50

SEPARATISM

RENÉ LÉVESQUE EDITORIAL CARTOON BY
DUNCAN MACPHERSON
Dec. 27, 1976

Opposite page
PRIME MINISTER PIERRE TRUDEAU WITH RENÉ LÉVESQUE AT THE CONSTITUTIONAL CONFERENCE
Ottawa, 1980

51

OUR PLACE IN THE WORLD

WORLD ON AZIMUTHAL EQUIDISTANT PROJECTION CENTRED NEAR WINNIPEG
July 1, 1943

[On an azimuthal equidistant map] directions and distances from the centre are correct. The centre can, of course, be anywhere on the earth and is often placed at the North Pole. On the map which accompanies this article it has been placed at a point between Brandon and Winnipeg. Such a map is startling, but surprisingly truthful. . . .

How does Canada fit into this picture? Our place is, if not in the middle, very close to it. The azimuthal projection shows at once that every direct route between North America and Europe or Asia crosses the Dominion.

— "Canada: mainstreet of the air," by Trevor Lloyd, July 1, 1943

We Canadians always seem to want to know what the rest of the world thinks of us, possibly because we're afraid that the rest of the world barely notices us—or worse, mistakes us for Americans. The 1943 article "Canada: mainstreet of the air" took the unusual approach of proving by azimuthal equidistant map that we are almost at the centre of everything.

WORLD on azimuthal equidistant projection centered near Winnipeg

World in Mercator projection Area of main map is red

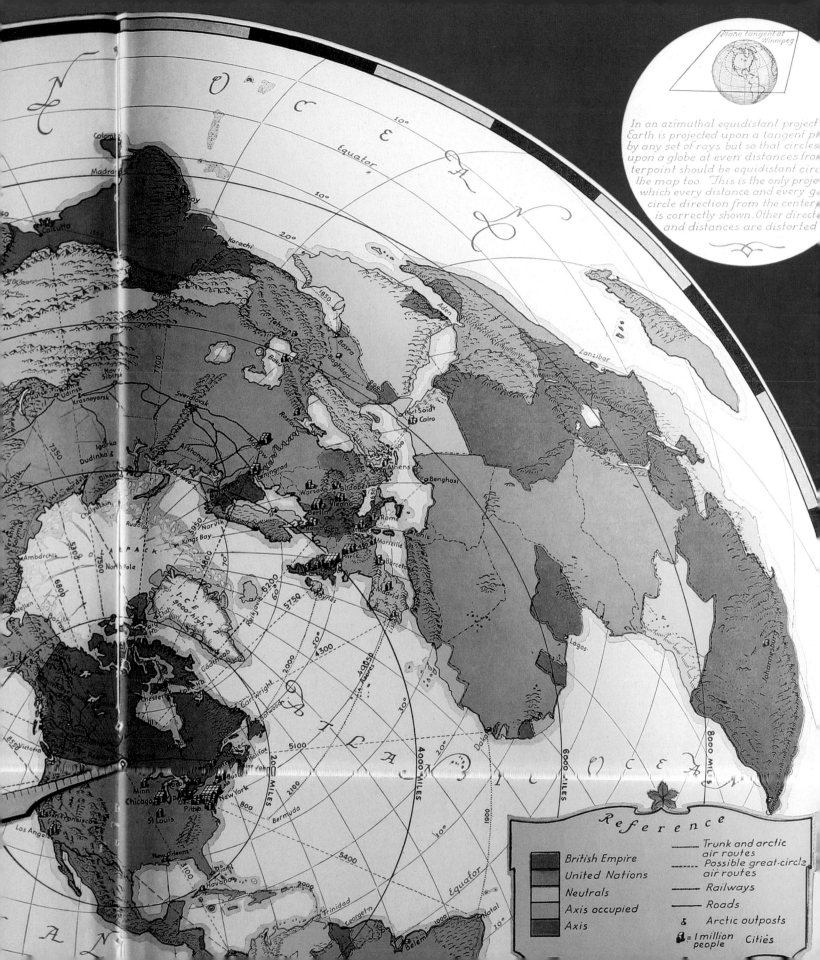

In an azimuthal equidistant projection
Earth is projected upon a tangent pl___
by any set of rays but so that circles___
upon a globe at even distances fro___
terpoint should be equidistant circ___
the map too. This is the only proje___
which every distance and every g___
circle direction from the center___
is correctly shown. Other direct___
and distances are distorted___

Plane tangent at
Winnipeg

Reference

■ British Empire	—— Trunk and arctic air routes
■ United Nations	------ Possible great-circle air routes
■ Neutrals	⊪⊪⊪ Railways
■ Axis occupied	—— Roads
■ Axis	⚓ Arctic outposts
	🏢 = 1 million people Cities

O C E A N
Equator
10°
10°
20°
1350
Aden
Zanzibar
Colomb
Madras
Bombay
Calcutta
Karachi
Tehran
Basra
Baghdad
Novo
Sibirsk
Udinsk
Krasnoyarsk
Sverdlovsk
Rostov
Port Said
Cairo
7700
Igarka
Dudinka
Arkhongel
Moscow
Warsaw
Budapest
Athens
Benghasi
7350
Diksono
Leningrad
Berlin
Vienna
Hamb
Rome
Tunis
Verkhi
Nordvik
Rudolph
Norvik
Marseille
Barcelona
Yakutsk
Kings Bay
North Pole
Paris
Ambarchik
5300
7500
6800
London
Madrid
Lagos
Wellen
ICE CAP
9000 high
Reykjavik
6200
6050
5750
Rennes
Chelyuskin
Nome
Boston
Godthaab
5900
Narvik
1960
800
5100
4300
4050
4000 MILES
Dako
Johannesburg
8000 MILES
6000 MILES
200 MILES
5100
2000
Cartwright
Cape Race
Chesterfield
Bartwood
Halifax
Victoria
6250
Point St John
Bermuda
Minn
Chicago
New York
Pitts
Buffalo
2100
800
St Louis
San Francisco
Los Angeles
New Orleans
Miami
Havana
5400
Trinidad
Georgetn
3100
2000
1000
A T L A N T I C   O C E A N
Equator
10°
20°
30°
40°
50°
Natal
Belém

THE MAGAZINE

The person who was supposed to write the essay for this page hasn't done so because history—quite literally—got in the way. Peter C. Newman still has a copy of a letter from *Maclean's* managing editor Pierre Berton, dated Oct. 13, 1954. In it, Berton acknowledged the acceptance, on behalf of editor Ralph Allen and himself, of Newman's first submission to the magazine. Just over 50 years later, as Peter was coming up to deadline to write a section opener for this book, we called him off: instead, he would write an essay for the magazine on Berton's passing at age 84—one Canadian literary legend bidding adieu to another, both of them with close ties to *Maclean's*.

The history and personality of *Maclean's* run parallel, in many ways, with the history and personality of the nation to which it is so indelibly tied—confident and purposeful at times, tentative and self-doubting at others.

Under Allen's editorship in the '50s, as Berton once wrote, "For any journalist, *Maclean's* . . . was the place to be." There were other similar periods under other editors when its leadership of the national agenda was also clear. But as Newman wrote, "In the early 1970s, *Maclean's* was running out of money, out of purpose and out of time." In a world of ever-changing conditions and snap decisions, it still plodded along as a monthly, increasingly lagging behind the national conversation. Publisher Lloyd Hodgkinson persuaded Newman to become its editor, and together they transformed it into a weekly newsmagazine.

The wisdom of that decision now seems clear, but at the time many thought it was foolhardy. And it *was* a big change. As Newman recalled in a 1995 essay: "Instead of sitting back calmly surveying the country's psyche and publishing elegant and occasionally witty jottings about the Canadian identity, the magazine began to run for office. By this I mean that we started seriously to compete for people's time and attention." That's been *Maclean's* goal, in various iterations and under a number of editors, ever since. Over the years, the speed with which we can receive information and the pace at which we live our lives have greatly intensified, but the desire of Canadians to learn different things about our country—and to look at ourselves in different ways—still burns with the same white heat. The big change in our approach as a newsweekly in recent years has been that we used to presume that the magazine would be the first point of access to news for many of our readers. But in a wired world in which access to news is instantaneous, a well-informed readership knows the basic elements surrounding major news events, so we build from that knowledge base. Readers look to *Maclean's* to hear more about Canada, and for a distinctively Canadian view of the world beyond our borders. One hundred years in, even as the world changes—as does the way we choose to cover it—that part of our mandate remains unaltered. Here's to another century of the same.

ANTHONY WILSON-SMITH (EDITOR, 2001-2005; JOINED *MACLEAN'S* STAFF IN 1983)

1 2 3 4 5 6 7 8 9 10 11 12 13 14 15 16 17 18 19 20 21 22 23 24 25 26 27
54 55 56 57 58 59 60 61 62 63 64 65 66 67 68 69 70 71 72 73 74 75 76

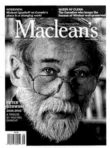

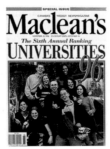

52

VIEWPOINTS

JUNE CALLWOOD
Toronto, 1957

"We are looking for geniuses," proclaimed a letter signed by "The Editors" in a 1910 issue of *Busy Man's Magazine*. "There is a risk in undertaking such a search and we are aware of the trouble-making temperament which is said to go hand in hand with genius. But . . . we need all the cleverest writers in Canada to make this magazine what we want it to be." John Bayne Maclean had grand ambitions for the periodical he had founded in 1905 and would rename after himself in 1911. Grand, but not completely unrealistic: by 1920, the bylines of Stephen Leacock, Lucy Maud Montgomery, Robert Service and Nellie McClung had all appeared in *Maclean's*.

During the editorships of William Arthur Irwin (1944-1949) and Ralph Allen (1949-1960), many of Canada's most respected journalists were on staff—Pierre Berton and Lionel Shapiro, for instance— or regular freelance contributors, such as June Callwood. Under editor Peter C. Newman, *Maclean's* became a newsmagazine in the late 1970s, and since then it has continued to evolve. But *Maclean's* is and has always been a forum for informed, opinionated Canadian voices. Today Ann Dowsett Johnston, Jonathon Gatehouse and Paul Wells are among those who share their views in its pages. And the search for up-and-coming genius wordsmiths never ends.

INDEX OF AUTHORS WHOSE WORK IS EXCERPTED IN THIS BOOK

this page (from top)
**EDITOR ANTHONY WILSON-SMITH
WHEN HE WAS *MACLEAN'S*
MOSCOW BUREAU CHIEF**
Moscow, 1988
***MACLEAN'S* WAR CORRESPONDENT
LIONEL SHAPIRO**
Sicily, circa 1943

INDEX OF PHOTOGRAPHERS WHOSE WORK APPEARS IN THIS BOOK

this page (from top)
MACLEAN'S PHOTOGRAPHERS
location unknown, circa 1915
**CHIEF PHOTOGRAPHER PETER BREGG WITH
PRIME MINISTER PAUL MARTIN**
Montreal, 2003
**GEORGE PIMENTEL WITH COMEDIAN
MIKE MYERS**
Los Angeles, 2003

53

IMAGES

YOUSUF KARSH WITH GLASS NEGATIVE
self-portrait, circa 1952

On neon-dazzled city nights and cloudless prairie days, in war zones and sports arenas and bedrooms, *Maclean's* photographers have captured countless indelible moments. Those affiliated with the magazine have included Don Newlands (photo editor, 1961-1965), Brian Willer (chief photographer, 1979-1993) and Peter Bregg (photo editor, 1990-2001; chief photographer since 2001). Yousuf Karsh also handled numerous *Maclean's* assignments. A 1942 profile of Karsh noted that he liked photographing pretty girls—provided their clothes had good lines—and that he regarded taking pictures of a friend's dog as two hours gone out of his life.

54

LINE AND COLOUR

CARTOONIST GEORGE FEYER
Toronto, 1956

The magazine's first covers were plain affairs, mere lines of type on coloured cardboard. Although illustrated covers had become the norm at *Maclean's* by 1911, in the early decades they varied wildly in quality, ranging from memorable works by Arthur Heming and A.J. Casson to generic images of demurely attractive women, cute kids and dogs.

During Eugene Aliman's reign as art director (1950-62), most *Maclean's* covers featured original artwork by an illustrator. The vivid storyteller Franklin Arbuckle, the sophisticated European émigré Oscar Cahén and the wryly observant Rex Woods were among Aliman's favourites. His successor—briefly—was Allan Fleming, one of Canada's most influential graphic designers. From the mid '60s to the 1990s, photography dominated *Maclean's* covers. However, current art director Donna Braggins has placed renewed emphasis on illustration.

Over the years, the magazine's cartoonists have included the whimsical George Feyer and gentle James Simpkins (creator of Jasper the bear, a *Maclean's* fixture from 1948 into the 1970s). Two of their more satirical counterparts, Duncan Macpherson and Roy Peterson, have contributed incisive political cartoons. So has Terry Mosher (Aislin), who is now *Maclean's* cartoon editor.

MACLEAN'S

"It's your turn to put out the cat."

INDEX OF ILLUSTRATORS AND CARTOONISTS WHOSE WORK APPEARS IN THIS BOOK

this page (from top)
JASPER CARTOON BY JAMES SIMPKINS
NOV. 15, 1949
OSCAR CAHÉN
near King City, Ont., 1951
**ILLUSTRATOR FRANKLIN ARBUCKLE
(RIGHT) WITH *MACLEAN'S* EDITOR RALPH
ALLEN ON ASSIGNMENT**
Saskatchewan or Alberta, July 1956

55

FICTION

**OPENING PAGE OF THE SHORT STORY
"AUNT ALICE'S HEART"**
July 1, 1936

"Old houses always make noises at night," she said. "Now let me read you to sleep, Aunt Alice. . . ."

Marty read a serious article as monotonously as possible, droning on with little attention to the words. . . .

And then the reading broke off, too short, with a wild intake of breath that would have come out in a scream but for her tight hand across her mouth. For under the bed, toward the foot, was a battered, blackened tan shoe. . . . Even as she stared, mind refusing to believe eyes, it was drawn noiselessly out of sight. . . .

—"Aunt Alice's heart," by Juliet Wilbor Tompkins, July 1, 1936

More than 1,500 short stories appeared in *Maclean's* over its first 50-odd years of publication. Some were by the likes of F. Scott Fitzgerald, W. Somerset Maugham and Morley Callaghan, but relatively inexpensive space fillers greatly outnumbered the timeless works of fiction.

From under the bed projected a foot in a battered shoe — Marty's hands turned to ice with fear.

By JULIET WILBOR TOMPKINS

In which the man under auntie's bed meets his match in the girl who loved the man next door

Aunt Alice's Heart

MARTY DROVE as though Aunt Alice were a consignment of frail glass. She slowed down for every bump and corner, she came to a full stop when told to, she let any kind of car pass. She had gone up yesterday in about three hours, but she was taking all day for the return trip. That was the way everyone treated Aunt Alice's heart. Marty could remember, years ago, when they took the slow, limited walks that the heart allowed, the fascinating importance it had had.

"Aunt Alice, if you ran up that tiny bit of a hill there, would you fall dead?" the little Marty would ask, and Aunt Alice, measuring the hill with a serious eye, would answer, "Yes, Marty, that hill would be enough." And, squeezing their hands in mutual satisfaction, they would go carefully around it, as one might skirt a bear's den.

Pete Gardiner, who lived next door then, used to say, "When I grow up, you bring your Aunt Alice to me; I'll cure her." Pete had inherited his profession as certainly as he had inherited blue eyes and red hair; but the Gardiner house had been rented or empty ever since the doctor died, and no one had been able to cure Aunt Alice.

Her yearly visit was a heavy responsibility. This year she had written that the train gave her palpitations, so Marty had polished her car and driven 110 miles to get her, missing the tournament for the West Coast championship. Marty was a little brown nut of a girl, not conspicuous for sentiment, but she had a doggy faithfulness to Aunt Alice.

"I think she is still expecting Aunt Alice to go bang any minute, and she likes the excitement," her father explained to her mother. "She wouldn't have cut that tennis match

for my funeral, you can bet. Yours, perhaps, but not mine." He always had private fits of laughter over Marty.

The morning passed uneventfully. They stopped for lunch, and, for a person who never took a step of exercise, Aunt Alice tucked in a very fair meal. After it she went comfortably to sleep. Marty's foot, restrained all day and sorely tried, finally took one moment's liberty with the gas. As they shot forward, a sport car that had been passing cut in ahead and there was a squeak of mudguard on bumper. Marty came to a careful stop. Aunt Alice's eyes were closed—but perhaps she had opened them and died of shock.

The car ahead had stopped and a young man came back.

"Any damage done?" he asked cheerfully, as though a near collision were a joke.

Aunt Alice certainly was breathing. Marty, badly shaken, got out to look at the car.

"You might have killed my aunt," she said in a bald undertone. "We never let anything jar or startle her because of her heart, and if you had run into us . . . ."

She felt rather than heard laughter. Looking up in outraged amazement, she saw mirthful blue eyes and hair that might be called mahogany.

"So Aunt Alice's heart is still on the job," said Pete Gardiner.

"Oh, hello, Pete." Marty's habit of understatement made her greeting casual. Her brown little paw offered an everyday sort of handshake. She had said good-by to him just like that nine years ago when he went east to be educated. If she cried afterward, no one ever knew it.

56

FACTS

STUDENT, NOVA SCOTIA COLLEGE OF ART AND DESIGN
Halifax, 2002

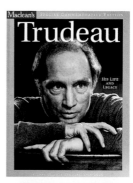

covers (from top)
TRUDEAU, HIS LIFE AND LEGACY (2000)
DIANA, HER LIFE AND LEGACY (1997)
LEADERS AND DREAMERS (2004)
MACLEAN'S GUIDE TO CANADIAN UNIVERSITIES (2004)

When it comes to your university years, a detour often leads you exactly where you're meant to go. So here is my advice: whether you're interested in film or physics, biology or architecture, take the time to find a school that fits, a place where you'll be comfortable exploring, both on and off the beaten path.

Finding the right fit is key, and the *Maclean's Guide to Canadian Universities* . . . is designed to help you do just that.
—"Introduction," *Maclean's Guide to Canadian Universities (2004)*, by Ann Dowsett Johnston

In addition to various special commemorative issues, *Maclean's* publishes two acclaimed education-related annuals: *Maclean's Guide to Canadian Universities* and a university rankings issue. Editor at large Ann Dowsett Johnston helms both post-secondary education projects.

QUALITIES

Canadian celebrity can seem like a contradiction in terms: famous Canadians tend to be modest, introspective, almost self-effacing. When I was growing up in the late 1950s, the most familiar voice in the country belonged to radio broadcaster Foster Hewitt. In hockey's golden age, when star athletes were paid like mere mortals, and the slapshot had yet to replace the wristshot, Hewitt's play-by-play stickhandling was the soundtrack to a Canadian sacrament. And despite Hewitt's obvious allegiance to the Leafs, the rise and fall of his even-handed, adenoidal drone served as a national telegraph, making us all equal observers in the neutral zone.

We are a land of circumspect icons. What other country could have produced Marshall McLuhan, an academic who became a household word by deconstructing the medium that made him famous? With some outrageous exceptions (Céline Dion), our stars distrust glitz and hype. They regard fame as a foreign currency prone to inflation, an endowment that should be viewed with suspicion, or at least an immunizing dose of irony. And in many cases—the Dionne Quints are an extreme example—Canadians don't choose celebrity so much as get chosen by it.

Our artists are a pantheon of iconoclasts, eccentrics, dissidents, misanthropes, explorers and émigrés. Leonard Cohen can vanish into a monastery on California's Mount Baldy for five years with no fear of losing his place. Glenn Gould turned his back on the stage and insulated his genius with gloves and overcoats. Mordecai Richler was an irascible renegade who turned himself into his favourite target. Rohinton Mistry sits in a small Ontario town and conjures up all of India on the page. David Cronenberg turns down studio thrillers and plants his existential flag on the most remote and chilling regions of the human psyche. Sarah Polley keeps her head above water in the Hollywood shark pool while rebelling against everything it stands for. And as our best-selling author, Margaret Atwood never forgets that she's a citizen of a culture at risk.

It's hard to put your finger on what constitutes integrity, but (like art, or obscenity) you know it when you see it. You recognize it in the birch timbre of Gordon Lightfoot's voice, in his honest songs that paint pictures and tell stories. You see it in the human curves of Raymond Moriyama's architecture, or in the architectural grace of Karen Kain's surrendering neck.

We are a country of complicated heroes, often of the tragic kind. Some are driven by an incandescent desire for justice. For Dr. Norman Bethune that meant travelling to China and joining Mao Tse-tung on the Long March. For Terry Fox it meant embarking on his one-legged Marathon of Hope. Both would die before completing their journeys, but that's because they chose insurmountable odds. They chose to let their personalties be overshadowed by the Work. Or in McLuhan's words, to let their medium be the message.

BRIAN D. JOHNSON (SENIOR WRITER; JOINED *MACLEAN'S* STAFF IN 1985)

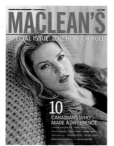

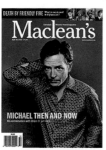

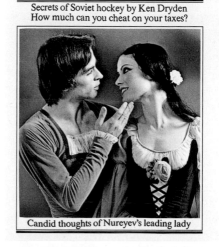

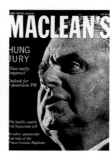

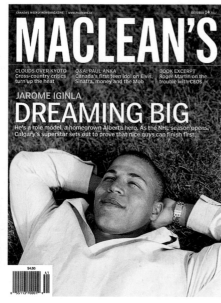

57

IDENTITY

FOSTER HEWITT BROADCASTING THE PLAY-BY-PLAY FOR A HOCKEY GAME AT MAPLE LEAF GARDENS
Toronto, circa 1950

Opposite page
ALANIS MORISSETTE
Los Angeles, 2002

Alanis *sounds* Canadian. She may have found paradise in California, where she kayaks, snowboards, plays basketball and practises yoga. But when she sings you can still hear Ottawa in the flattened curl of the letter "r."
—"Alanis in Wonderland," by Brian D. Johnson, Feb. 25, 2002

It is doubtful if more than a small fraction [of his] five million listeners would know Hewitt if they talked to him. His flamboyant voice with the trenchant tones of an evangelist belongs to an almost embarrassingly modest, retiring and colourless paradox.
—"Foster Hewitt, play-by-playboy," by Trent Frayne, April 1, 1950

The term "genius" is often used loosely to describe the exceptionally talented, but Gould was a genius in a more formal sense. Like Mozart and Einstein, he seemed to perceive the world in the light of an inner vision complete in itself. Gould's vision was composed of pure music, but his joy in it was qualified by the feeling that a piece of music exists perfectly in the mind and always imperfectly when it is actually played. However, he felt the effort was worthwhile. "The purpose of art," he wrote in 1962, "is the gradual lifelong construction of a state of wonder and serenity."

—"Glenn Gould, 1932–1982," by Mark Czarnecki, Oct. 18, 1982

[Cronenberg's] *The Fly* preys upon the midnight fear not that a stranger may be creeping up the stairs but that strangeness itself may be growing under the skin.

—"Creepy capers from a master of horror," by Brian D. Johnson, Aug. 25, 1986

Pianist Glenn Gould sought serenity through art; David Cronenberg's films provide ample evidence of art's power to disturb. But just as Gould's approach to music was probing and idiosyncratic, the cinematic master of psychological horror often feels compelled to defy movie-making conventions.

58

SINGULARITY

DAVID CRONENBERG
location unknown, 1996

Opposite page
GLENN GOULD
Toronto, 1974

59

MULTIPLICITY

THE DIONNE QUINTS WITH THEIR NURSES
location unknown, circa 1941

Opposite page
**THE DIONNE QUINTS "ROYAL TOUR" TRAIN
LEAVES UNION STATION**
Toronto, 1939

Although [Oliva and Elzire Dionne] are welcome to enter the hospital home of their five famous children and see them any time, they do not feel at ease there and stay away. . . . They are kept back by their helplessness to do anything, by the invisible barrier that runs between their small, poor house and the larger comfortable home of their five daughters across the road. . . . They cannot be convinced—even by those who have been inside the hospital and seen the ideally healthy, happy conditions under which those lucky little girls are being brought up—that their babies are safe.

"I saw the babies having their morning baths, being dressed and fed," I told Father Dionne. "They are so happy and well, and the nurses love them. There aren't any better-cared-for babies in the world than your five little daughters."

"Maybe they are getting good care," admitted the 32-year-old father. "But nurses, no matter how much they love the babies, can't take the place of a mother's love. Those babies should have their mother with them. Even pigs are allowed to bring up their own young," he added.

—"What's ahead for the Quints?" by Claire Wallace, Nov. 15, 1935

Canada's first quintuplets were born near North Bay, Ont., in 1934. After the Ontario government separated the girls from their impoverished parents and placed them in the custody of the doctor who had delivered them, Annette, Cécile, Émilie, Marie and Yvonne Dionne were raised in "Quintland," a nursery/compound built to show them off twice a day to tourists. Émilie died in 1954; Marie, in 1970. In 1998, the surviving three successfully sued for a share of Quintland profits.

60

VERVE

OSCAR PETERSON, "MONTREAL'S PHENOMENAL YOUNG SWINGSTER"
1945

Opposite page
DIANA KRALL
Washington, D.C., 2002

There is a slight difference of opinion between Oscar Peterson and the phonograph record makers. They say he plays hot jazz.

Oscar insists vehemently that his music is swing.

"Swing is sophisticated, grown-up jazz," he says. "I play swing."
—"Hot Piano," by Paul H. Zemke, Oct. 15, 1945

When is she happiest? "Every night," on stage, she says without hesitation. "When I'm doing something I can feel, and that I can personally relate to. When I'm playing with the musicians I'm playing with. It's the best part."
—"Krall comes home," by Paul Wells, April 26, 2004

Profiled nearly 60 years apart in *Maclean's*, 20-year-old Oscar Peterson and 39-year-old Diana Krall described their pride and joy in making music.

Decoration by W. Winter

HOT PIANO

"That Oscar Peterson plays the best ivory box I've ever heard," says Count Basie of Montreal's phenomenal young swingster

By Paul H. Zemke

TRAFFIC jammed and crowds gathered quickly in the downtown section of Montreal recently. Cops started clearing the people away; people who stood raptly, their eyes closed, their ears straining to follow the acrobatics of 10 black fingers on a piano keyboard in a music store.

"Swing," said a returned soldier. "Oh, boy—is that swing!"

"That's Oscar Peterson in there," his girl friend said. "I know his touch. I've got his records."

Yes, Oscar Peterson, Montreal's sensational negro swingster, son of a music-minded sleeping car porter, literally has stopped the traffic in the streets of his home city. He'd stop it elsewhere too, for he's the man of whom Count Basie—peer in the aristocracy of U. S. swing bandsmen—said, "That Oscar plays the best ivory box I've ever heard."

Jimmy Lunceford, another popular music maestro, heard Oscar give out with "Body and Soul."

"I like it," he said promptly. "I like it so well I'd like to take Peterson, 'Body and Soul,' to the States with me."

But Jimmy Lunceford did not take Oscar from Canada, for Peterson, along with Johnny Holmes, leader of Canada's No. 2 band and manager of the negro pianist, feels that there is a bright future in Canada for musicians.

"The talent is here now and our stuff is rapidly beginning to rival the best there is in the United States—with something special of our own to offer," says Oscar confidently.

Certainly Oscar Peterson has a style all his own. With his left hand he plays a "walking bass," or "boogie," and with his right a syncopated swing. In Oscar's case the right hand not only knows what the left is doing but approves and co-operates. The result is modern swing that reminds the hearer a little of Art Tatum, and yet is individual. Lester Young, swingster of note, shakes his head and says admiringly: "That man sure works up a storm on the piano."

Oscar is now 20 years old. He's modest, speaks softly. He doesn't drink. He stands two inches over six feet, and his 250 pounds is a hunk of smiling, engaging personality.

"I'd like it," he says shyly, "I sure would like it if I could be an example to the other young fellows coming into the music business."

Other musicians smile at this ambition. Oscar, they say, has long ago achieved it—even though he doesn't realize it.

He was tooting a trumpet in United Church concerts, given by William Thomas' band in Montreal, when he was five years old. *Continued on page 39*

Oscar Peterson — Prince of Swing

61

DETERMINATION

TERRY FOX ON HIS MARATHON OF HOPE
Toronto, July 1980

The hopping, running 22-year-old amputee was well over the halfway mark in his coast-to-coast odyssey.... From April 12, when he dipped his artificial limb into the Atlantic Ocean at St. John's and began his run, until last week and 5,342 km later, Terry Fox had become a national symbol of courage, and some close to him said even stubbornness.... [His run] ended on the Thunder Bay bypass headed for the Red River Road in Northern Ontario. For two days, maybe three, he hadn't felt right—but he wasn't about to quit. Then, at the 29-km point on Tuesday's run, he recalled, "There was a hardness of breath. I was coughing, I started to choke. I didn't know what was going on." ... People were lining the road ahead and he wanted to run out of people before he quit. "There was no way I was going to stop running, not with all those people there." So he ran another mile and then there were no people. And for Terry, no more road.
—"The agony and the ecstasy of Terry Fox," by Warren Gerard, Sept. 15, 1980

A recurrence of the cancer that had claimed Terry Fox's leg ended his run in 1980. By the time of his death, in June 1981, he had raised $24 million for the Canadian Cancer Society.

62
INTENSITY

LEONARD COHEN
Los Angeles, 2002

With Trudeau gone, you're the last cool international icon among your generation of Canadians—someone we'll forever associate with a Canada when everything seemed possible, when a bohemian intellectual could be prime minister and a Montreal poet could be world famous. . . .

There's enough lament for lost love on *Dear Heather* that it makes me wonder if it's a breakup album. But in a sense, they're all breakup albums, aren't they? Whether you take us to the end of love, or the end of time, you like to dwell on what you once called *the crack in everything / That's how the light gets in.* Illumination and Armageddon joined at the hip.
—"Letter to Leonard," by Brian D. Johnson, Oct. 11, 2004

In the fall of 2004, Leonard Cohen turned 70 and released his 14th studio album, *Dear Heather*. He declined to do interviews to promote the recording, saying that it spoke for itself. *Maclean's* senior writer Brian D. Johnson, who has interviewed Cohen on several other occasions, couldn't persuade the bard of emotional and sonic profundity to change his mind on this one. Johnson subsequently wrote "Letter to Leonard," which contains the phrase, "This is not a review; it's a fan letter."

63

VISION

ARCHITECT RAYMOND MORIYAMA
Toronto, 1999

Opposite page
AUTHOR MARGARET ATWOOD
Toronto, 2003

A private man, spiritual—and a great storyteller—Moriyama wants his buildings to exude these same qualities. And they certainly can be found—in the slow dance of the setting sun along the curved museum wall in the Saudi Arabian desert; or in the quietude of the Canadian ambassador's office in Tokyo, tucked away under sloping steel rafters like a high-tech tree house. All private vistas, even in the most communal of settings.

—*Maclean's* Honour Roll profile of Raymond Moriyama, by Robert Sheppard, Dec. 13, 1999

"We're both saved and doomed by hope—'dirty hope,' Camus called it. It keeps us going and it keeps us blind to reality." Humans, the author believes, can turn anything to good or evil. "The problem with us is we have two hands."

—Margaret Atwood, quoted in "Atwood apocalyptic," by Brian Bethune, April 28, 2003

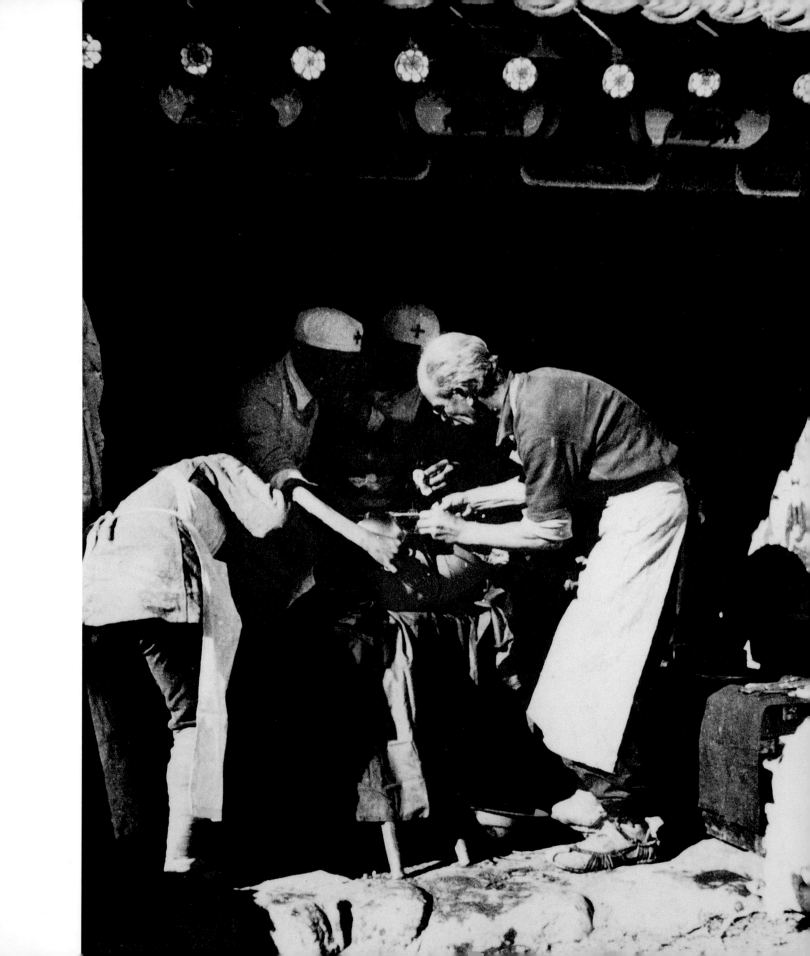

Even the stoic Chinese had never seen anything like the tireless pace he set. . . . "Go to the wounded. Don't wait for the wounded to come to you," he told them and, with a caravan which included a portable operating theatre, he set out for the Wutai Mountains where the Japanese were attacking.
—"The only Canadian the Chinese ever heard of," by Anne MacDermot, May 19, 1962

When he paints, he attacks his canvas with violent jabs and sweeps and the paint goes on in pre-shaped wedges, layer upon layer, spasm after spasm.
—"The native genius we've never discovered," by Catherine Jones, Aug. 3, 1957

Long before Canadians claimed him as a hero, Chinese Communists revered Montreal doctor Norman Bethune for his frontline contributions to their cause during Japan's late-1930s invasion of China. Another Montrealer, abstraction ist painter Jean-Paul Riopelle, achieved his greatest fame after moving to Paris.

64

NONCONFORMITY

PAINTER JEAN-PAUL RIOPELLE
location unknown 1965

Opposite page
DR. NORMAN BETHUNE PERFORMING FIELD SURGERY
China, 1939

65

ELOQUENCE

MORDECAI RICHLER
Toronto, 1958

Opposite page
ROHINTON MISTRY
Toronto, 2002

When I returned to Canada in 1951 after two years of wandering in Europe, my father took me out for a drive.

"I hear you wrote a novel in Europe," he said.

"Yes."

"What's it called?"

"*The Acrobats*," I told him.

For the next five minutes, we drove in silence. Then, he said, "What in the hell do you know about the circus?"

I explained that the title was a symbolic one. And, after another 10 minutes of uneasy silence, my father asked me, "Is it about Jews or ordinary people?"

I told him that it was about both.

"Well," he said, "you're no longer a kid. I guess you ought to start thinking about getting a job."

—"How I became an unknown with my first novel," by Mordecai Richler, Feb. 1, 1958

Above, an excerpt from Mordecai Richler's first *Maclean's* article; Rohinton Mistry found his literary voice after moving from India to Canada.

66

HUMOUR

STEPHEN LEACOCK IN HIS LIBRARY
Orillia, Ont., 1942

The dozens of *Maclean's* articles that Stephen Leacock wrote between 1915 and 1943 reflected his dual status as a humourist and a professor of economics—his subjects ranged from the perils of public speaking to the financial consequences of the First World War. (The photo above is by Yousuf Karsh.)

It is much harder to write one of Owen Seaman's "funny" poems in Punch than to write one of the Archbishop of Canterbury's sermons. Mark Twain's *Huckleberry Finn* is a greater work than Kant's *Critique of Pure Reason*, and Charles Dickens' creation of Mr. Pickwick did more for the elevation of the human race—I say it in all seriousness—than Cardinal Newman's *Lead Kindly Light Amid the Encircling Gloom*. Newman only cried out for light in the gloom of a sad world. Dickens gave it.

—"Humour as I see it," by Stephen Leacock, May 1916

Joey is 48, a 132-pound, five-foot-five-inch bundle of restless and apparently inexhaustible energy. There's just a fleck of grey to the black hair that sweeps back from a high forehead, from which it has also begun to recede. The furrowed lines across the brow, the sharp wedge of the nose, the eyes that narrow in concentration and the thin, malleable lips that can smile tightly, twist speculatively or purse expressively as he speaks, were all concocted by some good fairy who knew this man was going to stand on platforms and who plotted that no listener should be able to look away.

—"The Smallwood saga," by Gerald Anglin, Aug. 15, 1949

Newfoundland had officially been part of Canada for mere months when Gerald Anglin's profile of Premier Joey Smallwood appeared in *Maclean's*. Many Newfoundlanders had wanted to remain independent, but Smallwood convinced a slim majority of voters to "choose Canada" in the 1948 confederation referendum.

67

PERSUASIVENESS

JOEY SMALLWOOD
Newfoundland, 1965

68

EXPRESSIVENESS

**NATIONAL BALLET OF CANADA
FOUNDER CELIA FRANCA**
Montreal, 1955

Opposite page
GORDON LIGHTFOOT
Unionville, Ont., 1971

Celia Franca opened a summer school for dancers at St. Lawrence Hall, above Toronto's venerable city market. During the winter the hall is used as a sleeping place for transients and a musty smell still lingered about it, mingling with the seasonal odors of fruit and vegetables. The great old hall with its peeling paint and high vaulted ceilings still suggests those days of grandeur when Jenny Lind, the Swedish Nightingale, sang there. . . . But Celia Franca's dancers gave it a new life.
—"A great ballet star gambles on Canada," by Ken Johnstone, Aug. 20, 1955

He went from singing in a bar to filling Vancouver's Queen Elizabeth Theatre in a matter of months. . . . He composed honest tunes with an astonishing variety of textures. His lyrics are straightforward and touching, without obscurantism or flatulent philosophy.
—"Gordon Lightfoot," by Marjorie Harris, September 1968

In 1955, *Maclean's* noted that British ballet star Celia Franca's decision to found a classical dance company in Canada was "like Hap Day quitting the Leafs for the minor leagues." Today, the National Ballet is a great Canadian institution. As is Gordon Lightfoot.

69

ACUMEN

K.C. IRVING
location unknown, 1950s

Opposite page
ESKANDAR AND NADER GHERMEZIAN AT THE WEST EDMONTON MALL
Edmonton, 1986

His personal manners bear so little resemblance to his corporate manners that some of the people who have seen him lose his temper . . . have put it down to business tactics rather than blood pressure. During my four meetings with him I saw the polite Irving only: the same Irving his loggers, his clerks and his foremen see, the Irving in whom old-fashioned courtesy appears to be as deeply imbedded as his Presbyterian code of morals. Although, in the course of duty, I felt I had to ask him two or three rude questions, he never offered a rude answer:

Q: It has been said, by people who think they know, that you are worth between $300 million and $400 million. Have you any comment?

A: I have no comment whatsoever.

—"The art of wielding power: K.C. Irving (part three)," by Ralph Allen, May 16, 1964

New Brunswick's K.C. Irving founded a diversified corporate empire; Alberta's Ghermezian family owns the West Edmonton Mall and Minnesota's almost-as-huge Mall of America.

70

GRACE

NATIONAL BALLET OF CANADA PRINCIPAL DANCER KAREN KAIN AND GUEST ARTIST RUDOLF NUREYEV
location unknown, 1974

A recipient of the Governor General's Award for Lifetime Achievement, Karen Kain danced with the National Ballet from 1969 until 1997. In 2004, she was appointed chair of the Canada Council for the Arts.

Karen Kain, at 23, is notable as Canada's foremost young female dancer; to me, she is especially memorable as the only dancer I've met who restored my lack of faith in human nature. The only one to talk honestly about her profession; demythologized, without platitudes and bunk. . . .

"My life isn't exciting. It's not profitable. It's just mine. Usually I get home dead tired. I share an apartment with a sister in Toronto, when I'm not on tour. I grab something to eat, the first thing handy, then have a bath, do some laundry, or mend my shoes, watching television for a while, Johnny Carson. Then the next day starts, the same routine."
—"Lifting the curtain on the National Ballet," by John Hofsess, April 1974

It is as much a *way* of thinking as a body of thought. And to enter McLuhan's world can be a very comforting experience.

For one thing, McLuhanism can be used to interpret anything, from the Beatles to Plato, from Cézanne to the Chinese bomb. For another, McLuhan draws much of his subject matter from the artifacts of pop culture—and nothing could possibly be more endearing to your 1965 intellectual than a newly minted theory that makes Batman, Andy Warhol and the Rolling Stones all seem *meaningful*. Finally, McLuhanism is a hopeful creed. Instead of despairing at man's fate in a new line-dominated world, McLuhan sees electronic technology as Western man's salvation—the means by which he will regain his psychic unity.

—"The high priest of pop culture," by Alexander Ross, July 3, 1965

When Alexander Ross profiled him in 1965, University of Toronto professor Marshall McLuhan had been the director of the Centre for Culture and Technology for two years. Outside Canada, Ross wrote, McLuhan was already an 'ism', with the potential to become "the hottest intellectual fad since Zen Buddhism."

71

INSIGHT

MARSHALL MᶜLUHAN, WITH RENÉ CERA'S 1969 WORK *PIED PIPERS ALL*
Toronto, 1969

72

COMMITMENT

SARAH POLLEY
Toronto, 2003

Opposite page
JAROME IGINLA
Calgary, 2002

A lot of people were surprised by Iginla's dominance last season. They shouldn't have been. He decided at age 7 he was going to make it to the NHL, after one of his very first games. . . .

When he reached the NHL, coaches said his skating ought to be better, so he addressed that. "I approach it like a sprinter, trying to get more explosive," Iginla says of the specialized regimen. Last season, the team needed him to score more, so instead of passing in certain situations, he began to shoot. Bingo, more goals.
—"The real-life dreams of Jarome Iginla," by James Deacon, Oct. 14, 2002

Committed to his sport, Calgary Flames right winger Jarome Iginla also makes time for charity work. Sarah Polley, who balances acting with political activism, once told *Maclean's:* "I don't think it's ever a bad idea for anyone to express an opinion."

EPHEMERA

It's paynight in boomtown, and the symbols of prosperity are everywhere. Electric light spills from windows along Main Street, while neon tavern signs hold out the promise of strong drink. A web of utility wires fans out overhead, and late-model sedans line the sidewalk in front of a cleaning store. Kirkland Lake, a gold-mining town in northern Ontario, was an anomaly during the Great Depression. But like all booms, its glory days petered out, and a single scene from that time is curiously absorbing today: this, evidently, is what it meant to have money in 1938. Electricity. Telephones. Professionally cleaned clothes. Maybe enough cash for a night on the town.

Such fleeting images give history its texture—though we seldom realize it at the time. Some work subtly, like the scene inside a men's club in the '50s (notice the hunched figure in the foreground leaning over his beer as if in prayer). Others scream out, like the floral pattern on Pierre Trudeau's shirt in 1971.

The measure of their relevance is not in their durability, or their sensationalism, but in how they converse with official history. We know, for example, that outside contact permanently altered life in the Far North. But where has it been more graphically illustrated than inside the igloo *Maclean's* visited in 1949? The scene must have seemed a whimsical juxtaposition of cultures at the time—like the magazine cut-outs stuck to the igloo's icy walls. Today, it registers as the genesis of a social catastrophe, tragically symbolized by current images of children slumped over plastic bags, inhaling fumes of gasoline. Anyone who has seen the latter can't help but look on the former with sorrow.

No editor knows for certain which pictures will resonate, of course. And as a country born in the photographic age, Canada is awash in its own imagery, meaning it takes a pretty special image to rise above the fray. The result is a marked prejudice in favour of the icon, the Last Spike-style photo that will stand the test of the ages, landing in schoolbooks for generations to come. The back stories to those images can make compelling narrative. (Who chose that spike in Craigellachie, B.C.? Was that really water in Sir John A. Macdonald's glass?) But as artifacts these official portraits of a nation are limited.

More illuminating is the imagery not intended for posterity, like an ad for the latest appliance fad, or laundry strung above the dirt in one of Canada's first suburbs. In them, we can see daily life writ large—its pleasures, frustrations, triumphs and banalities. Their contents shift with our priorities, and often as not these images slip past unnoticed. But it's impossible to view them without seeing some small part of ourselves. It might be the glow emanating from a newly crowned beauty queen. Or weariness on the face of an immigrant labourer. It's the stuff that gives history its colour, even when captured in black and white.

CHARLIE GILLIS (NATIONAL CORRESPONDENT; JOINED *MACLEAN'S* STAFF IN 2003)

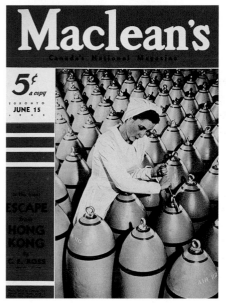

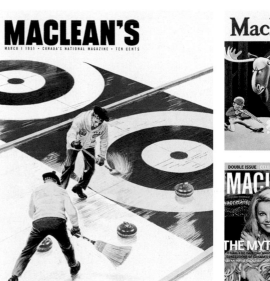

73

COMMUNITY

UKRANIAN CHILDREN PLAYING
location unknown, circa 1930

Opposite page
MEN'S CLUB
Toronto, circa 1955

A 1956 profile of grocer and radio show producer Johnny Lombardi, excerpted at right, captured the vitality of Toronto's Little Italy; the majority of the 240,000 Ukrainians who immigrated to Canada between 1891 and 1939 settled in the Western provinces.

[Radio announcers Ontario Sarracini, Aldo Maggiorotti and Dedena Morello] may urge their listeners to patronize Mario's Spaghetti House, to cook only with olive oil prepared by Gattuso . . . to drink Caffe Roma, to relax at the Italo-Canadian Recreation Club, to read the Corriere Canadese and to make the long-cherished trip to the old country a memorable one in a ship of the Italian Line.

Barbers in the audience may be urged to join the Italian local of the barbers' union, and the ladies—"regardless of age"—urged to make an appointment at Mary's Beauty Salon where "Mary Greico, her lovely and talented daughter Dolores and the rest of the staff . . . will give you personal and patient attention."

—"Johnny Lombardi's kingdom of music and macaroni," by Richard O'Hagan, Dec. 8, 1956

74

NIGHTLIFE

HOUSE OF HAMBOURG JAZZ CLUB
Toronto, 1957

Opposite page
MAIN STREET ON PAYNIGHT
Kirkland Lake, Ont., 1938

Who'd have believed that Canada, thought of by foreigners and often by ourselves as a staid and frigid country, would become one of the world's great centres of hot jazz? Yet that's exactly what's happening. Jazz musicians are flocking north of the border to garner as much as $14,000 a week—big money even on New York terms. Canadian jazz musicians are touring the world. One Canadian city, Montreal, now has 200 nightclubs, more than Chicago and Los Angeles combined, most of them dedicated to jazz in one form or another.
—"Backstage" item, Sept. 14, 1957

The street scene photo ran in "Mine-money triangle," a 1938 article that described three Ontario mining communities—Timmins, Sudbury and Kirkland Lake—as islands of prosperity in the Depression. At left is a photo from "The jazz-happy tailor," a 1957 article. It profiled Toronto man-about-town David Caplan, clothier to musicians and other local celebrities. That's him and his cigarette in the foreground.

[A] half-million families . . . have moved into the suburbs of Canadian cities in the last eight years in a migration unparallelled in our history. These half-million families are new pioneers on an old frontier—the home front. Their battles against traffic, mud, loneliness, blocked septic tanks and rising taxes are part of a changing pattern of Canadian living. By the year 2000, according to Eugene Faludi, a prominent town-planning consultant, "half the population will live in houses built in a rural atmosphere so there is room to breathe and see the sun."

—"Why live in the suburbs?" by John Gray, Sept. 1, 1954

In 1954, *Maclean's* reported that "two trends and a machine" were behind the postwar suburban boom. The trends were a burgeoning population and a readiness to forsake farm life for a job in the city; the machine was, of course, the car.

75

SUBURBIA

EIGHTY UNITS OF TWO-STOREY HOUSES UNDER CONSTRUCTION
Hamilton, June 1959

Opposite page
CLOTHESLINE
location unknown, 1950s

76

COMPETITION

RIDING A BRONC AT THE CALGARY STAMPEDE
Calgary, 1980

Opposite page
BILLIE HALLAM, 17, BEGINS HER REIGN AS MISS TORONTO OF 1937
Toronto, 1937

There is no way for someone to sit a horse or a bull for eight seconds (or 10, when that's called for) without taking a lot of cruel and unusual punishment. Every rider—successful or instantly thrown—suffers disorientation on touching ground. A sine wave passes through a man's body, not smoothly but powerfully, whiplashing both ends against the humped-up, bucked and belted middle. That kind of violence sends shocks against the brain pan as severe, it seems to me, as a succession of uppercuts on the chin of a boxer. . . .

Think of the difficulty one has trying to figure an electric maze of complexity and trickiness: a bucking surging bronc or wildly spinning bull of the championship class is far more difficult to figure than a maze, and eight seconds, which, as punishment, may seem a century, is, as time allowed for problem-solving, incredibly short."
—"Get an outfit, be a cowboy," by Jack Ludwig, July 1975

77

DOMESTICITY

AD FOR INTERNATIONAL HARVESTER'S "DECORATOR REFRIGERATOR"
March 1, 1953

Opposite page
INSIDE IGLOO
Northern Quebec, 1949

That first night I tried to follow the others in getting my clothes off as quickly as possible without scattering snow about. In underwear and socks I crawled feet first into my caribou fur sleeping bag which in turn was inside my eiderdown bag and this in turn inside a canvas wrapper. And I was just as cold as you'd expect to be inside a canvas tent at 60 below. But in two minutes I was as warm as I've been under an electric blanket in a steam-heated penthouse.

—"We went baby-hunting in the Arctic," by Richard Harrington with Gerald Anglin, Dec. 15, 1949

Richard Harrington, who took the photo at far left, made a 1,600-km dogsled trek through Canada's Far North in 1949; four years later and considerably farther south, the drapery-matching fridge was a marketing concept that never quite caught on.

78

ENCOUNTERS

**CHARLIE CHAMBERLAIN WITH
SCHOOLCHILDREN**
Halifax, 1965

After he got out of the fifth grade he headed for the woods and became a lumberjack. In the logging camps at night the men would gather around a stepdancing platform improvised from barrel staves. Someone had a mouth organ, someone else banged a spike on a horseshoe and Chamberlain strummed a battered guitar and sang in a fine clear voice that filled the forests. . . .

One day in 1934 an accountant from Saint John, Lansdowne Belyea, was riding on the CNR's Ocean Limited when he heard Chamberlain in the smoking car, plunking away on a two-string guitar and singing. . . .

Belyea, sensing that Chamberlain had a potentially fine voice, sent him to a singing teacher. She began showing him how to shape his mouth.

"Lookit here, lady," he said finally. "If I start thinking about the words they won't come out. Good day."

Chamberlain's voice, which grew in the great backwoods, was meant to be as free as, say, the call of a moose.
—"The breakdown boys from Spud Island," by David MacDonald, Oct. 15, 1953

Bathurst, N.B.'s own Charlie Chamberlain had just one brief encounter with a singing teacher, but the "lumberjack vocalist" became a beloved entertainer with Don Messer and his Islanders.

Loyal citizens
do not hoard

RATIONED
SUGAR ½lb. a week
PER PERSON
TEA ½ of the usual
PURCHASE
COFFEE 3/4 of the
USUAL PURCHASE

79

THE HOME FRONT

WW2 RATIONING
location unknown, circa 1943

Opposite page
JUNE 15, 1942 COVER PHOTO
"500-LB. BOMBS MADE IN CANADA"
location unknown, 1942

Even under rationing the housekeeper who likes to exercise her ingenuity and her skill along thrifty lines can feed her family very well indeed. . . .

Of course it will take more planning, more juggling and more figuring with the menu jigsaw, more careful shopping to get the meat value for your coupon, more knowledge of cuts and their uses, more skilful seasoning than it did under the old system of a big roast on Sunday, cold sliced on washday and a succession of chops, steaks and cutlets the rest of the week. But why worry—isn't half the fun of our housekeeping job to lick each problem we meet and turn it to our advantage?
—"With a little meat," by Helen G. Campbell, May 15, 1943

A recipe for Oatmeal Beef-Liver Loaf was one of the meat-stretching menu ideas that ran with the article above.

Society's symbol of success has become the $10,000-a-year job. ...
When a man lands a job with a salary of at least $10,000—or, as happens
more often, is promoted to a $10,000 job—he has won entry into the
inner circle. Not only does he gain prestige as a successful provider for
his family and respect as a substantial member of the community ...
he also becomes a member of society's dominant group.

Before the Second World War, the symbol was the $5,000-a-year job.
Today the sum has doubled, and the symbol itself has taken on an
extra sheen. Says Professor John Morgan, of the University of Toronto's
School of Social Work, "The growing tendency to judge a man by the
amount of money he makes is a simple fact of life."

—"$10,000: Everybody's target and how to hit it," by Roy Shields, July 16, 1960

In 1960 any man with a
$10,000-a-year job was in
an enviable position—and
few women even dared to
dream of making that
much. It's safe to say that
the telephone operators
in the photo at left made
considerably less than
that. And they probably
didn't get foosball breaks.

80

WORK

"TOP 100 EMPLOYERS" COVER PHOTO,
TAKEN AT METSO AUTOMATION
Calgary, 2002

Opposite page
TELEPHONE SWITCHBOARD OPERATORS
Ottawa, circa 1950

81

LEISURE

URBAN GOLF
Toronto, 2004

Opposite page
SWIMMING AT THE CHÂTEAU LAURIER
Ottawa, 1954

A small army of trendsetters—equipped with second-hand drivers—is waging a war on golf. Tired of snooty country-club attitudes, goofy clothes and expensive green fees, they're taking the game to the street—hitting balls down fairways lined with cars, on greens flanked by office buildings and at garbage bins and fire hydrants that serve as holes.
—"Street tigers," by John Intini, Aug. 2, 2004

Pursuing familiar pastimes in unfamiliar settings is a human compulsion. Urban golf is catching on; hotels with indoor pools were news in the 1950s.

Hugh MacLennan: Two solitudes too long
Pleasures and perils of the new promiscuity
Farley Mowat: Advertisements for myself

AUGUST 1971 CANADA'S NATIONAL MAGAZINE 35¢

Maclean's

The great Russian road show, starring Margie and Pierre

82

STYLE

**PIERRE AND MARGARET TRUDEAU
IN THE SOVIET UNION**
Maclean's cover, August 1971

Opposite page
**JACK CREED ADJUSTS A FUR COAT ON
MODEL NOREEN MᶜNERNY**
Toronto, 1950

For the women on the [1971 state visit
by Pierre and Margaret Trudeau],
impressions of the U.S.S.R. may well be
forever entangled with memories of
distinguished political commentators
sidling up to them in places like the
Armory Museum within the Kremlin
wall and saying, "Would it be fair to
say that what she's wearing is a teal-
blue midi bound in beige?"
—"Our heroes on the Russian Front," by
Christina Newman (now Christina McCall),
August 1971

In 1971, fashion-forward newlyweds
Margaret and Pierre Trudeau could
get away with looking resplendently
bohemian on a state visit to the Soviet
Union. Quite a change from what had
been the regal pinnacle of chic two
decades earlier, a 1950 article on furrier
Jack Creed noted that figure skater
Barbara Ann Scott "sports a Creed's
natural ermine coat, an ermine jacket
and a silver mink cape."

RECURRING THEMES

"Canadians are forever taking the national pulse like doctors at a sickbed: the aim is not to see whether the patient will live well, but simply whether he will live at all."
—Margaret Atwood, *Survival*

Our self-regard may be a little too tortured to qualify as narcissism, but we Canadians certainly aren't averse to staring at our own reflections. For the better part of two centuries, we've poked, prodded, studied and debated the things that make us who we are. And yet, somehow, we never manage to reach a full consensus.

Some of it's easy, as obvious as high mountains, wide prairie skies, churning seas, and hockey on a Saturday night. We long ago opted for peace, order and good government, mounties instead of gunslingers, co-operation over confrontation. We've fallen in love with the notion that our soldiers make peace, not war. And we're fiercely proud of, if a little worried about, a health system built on the ideal that proper medical care is a right, not a privilege.

Our country is so vast and varied that it can frequently seem like we are five, 10, or 20 nations instead of one. But the great national tests—wars, economic depressions, disasters, both natural and man-made—have been repeatedly passed. Our politicians may bicker, but in the face of true threats and tragedies, the distances and divisions between us fade.

As citizens of the only country in the world that defines itself by what it's not—the United States of America—most Canadians are convinced that our way of doing things is superior, but vague as to why that is. There's our healthy skepticism about our leaders and government—a not-too-hot, not-too-cold compromise between blind faith and total disillusionment. Our growing belief that our cultural fabric is richer because it's a quilt, rather than a whole piece of cloth. The quiet pride in our history and traditions (although we seem to have outgrown our once abiding fascination with royalty.) And our pervasive distrust of extremes in all facets of society.

We believe in rights, but subject to "reasonable" limitations. Our national priorities are domestic—education, health, social services, the environment—yet we don't just look inward. Canadian businesses, athletes, entertainers and artists find success on the global stage. We know how to take a joke, and make one, keeping the rest of the world amused with our ability to laugh at ourselves.

The themes are familiar. One of the fascinating things about our history is how constant our national aspirations have remained, how predictable our points of friction have become. Yet Canada has changed, evolved and altered in a million ways that no one could have foreseen. Yes, our journey of self-discovery is endless. But maybe that's because what we see in the mirror today is never quite the same as it was yesterday.

JONATHON GATEHOUSE (NATIONAL CORRESPONDENT; JOINED *MACLEAN'S* STAFF IN 2001)

1 2 3 4 5 6 7 8 9 10 11 12 13 14 15 16 17 18 19 20 21 22 23 24 25 26 27
54 55 56 57 58 59 60 61 62 63 64 65 66 67 68 69 70 71 72 73 74 75 76

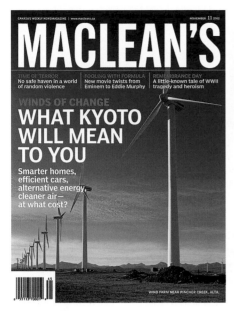

30 31 32 33 34 35 36 37 38 39 40 41 42 43 44 45 46 47 48 49 50 51 52 53
79 80 81 82 **83 84 85 86 87 88 89 90 91 92 93 94 95 96 97 98 99 100**

The Canadians scorched the Olympic Stadium track, leaving the favoured Americans well behind. So much so that Bailey, running the anchor leg, eased up and raised a finger signifying No. 1 as he crossed the finish line. The Canadians then circled the track again, slowly, joyously, and wrapped in the Maple Leaf flag. "This is better than [winning] the 100," a grinning Bailey said before the medal ceremony, "because . . . my teammates have big smiles on their faces, too. We are going to go out there, listen to the Canadian anthem, look to the sky and it's golden."

—"Best in the world," by Mary Nemeth, Aug. 12, 1996

At the 1996 Olympic Games in Atlanta, Donovan Bailey won the men's 100-m race—in the record time of 9.84 seconds—several days before he and teammates Bruny Surin, Glenroy Gilbert and Robert Esmie triumphed in the 4 x 100-m relay.

83
ALLEGIANCE

ARMISTICE DAY
Wakeham Bay, Que., 1927

Opposite page
**DONOVAN BAILEY (RIGHT) AND
BRUNY SURIN**
Austin, Texas, 2000

84

Stocks or slots? Either way, the players are willing to risk some money in the hope of making more.

MONEY

POSTING THE LATEST STOCK QUOTATIONS AT FRANK S. LESLIE & CO.
Toronto, 1959

Opposite page
CASINO PATRONS, AKWESASNE RESERVE
near Cornwall, Ont., circa 1990

The [Toronto Stock] Exchange offers a channel through which private savings can flow into new production—from motor cars to baby buggies, canned goods to gold.

It is also the biggest gambling joint in the country, where manipulators with half a million for play can "make a market" in a mining stock to lure in the little men, then unload for a killing when the price is right. Where insiders of mighty enterprises can split old shares three ways and (in politer language) "take a profit" when the resultant flurry of interest among new buyers has boosted the new and more numerous issue above the old presplitting level. Where Grandma and a hundred thousand amateurs like her can take a daring flier, then panic at some unexpected drop and turn it into an avalanche, carrying the market and their own modest fortunes into the dustbin.
—"Bull market," by Gerald Anglin, June 15, 1946

Parents [who participated in a 2002 *Maclean's/Today's Parent* poll] offered a litany of complaints about public school systems across the country—from large classes to poor discipline and a dearth of programs for students with special needs. In parents' minds, cutbacks to education—at every level—pose a real threat to their children's ability to survive in a competitive marketplace. . . .

Some parents complain that they are forced to pick up the slack as teachers scramble to keep up with large classes and changes in the curriculum. "Teachers can't cover all the material in the classroom," says Debbie Kurcz of Windsor, Ont., whose children are in Grades 10, 7 and 4. "They are under a lot of pressure. It's, 'OK, here's your multiplication tables, do this at home.' I find I'm doing the teaching."

—"What parents don't know (or won't admit)", by Sharon Doyle Driedger, Sept. 30, 2002

Maclean's **art director Donna Braggins recalls why she chose Toronto artist Gary Taxali to illustrate a 2002 poll-based cover story on kids and their parents: "Illustration's universality can represent a poll's breadth of opinion, and Gary's wonderful naive style suits the subject."**

85

EDUCATION

RAILWAY CLASSROOM
location unknown, circa 1925

Opposite page
ILLUSTRATION FOR "WHAT PARENTS DON'T KNOW" COVER
Sept. 30, 2002

86

ENVIRONMENT

**GARBAGE AT THE KEELE VALLEY
LANDFILL SITE**
Vaughan, Ont., May 2002

By the early 21st century, huge quantities of waste were crossing the Canada/ U.S. border in both directions. With existing landfills close to home maxxed out, Toronto and other Ontario centres made controversial arrangements to ship their garbage to Michigan. Simultaneously, sites in Ontario and Quebec were serving as dumping grounds for U.S. hazardous waste. Most sobering of all is the fact that taking out the trash is only one of many pressing environmental issues on this planet.

As of January [2003], Canada's largest city won't have anywhere nearby to dump its refuse.

At the 20-year-old Keele Valley Landfill Site, just north of Toronto, heaps of garbage tower 10 storeys above the ground. It's full and the province is shutting it down. A plan to solve the dilemma by shipping the city's dreck 600 km north by rail to an abandoned iron-ore mine near Kirkland Lake derailed when the city and the dump's prospective operator couldn't reach agreement. So starting in 2003 Toronto will truck its garbage, about a million tonnes a year, to a dump in Michigan. That's about 120 packed transport trucks making the 11-hour round trip down busy Highway 401, through populous Southwestern Ontario, each day. . . . The dump closure, says Geoff Rathbone, director of policy and planning with Toronto's division of solid waste management, "is causing us to rethink how we manage garbage."

—"Garbage" sidebar, by Danylo Hawaleshka, in the July 29, 2002 cover package, "Fouling our cities"

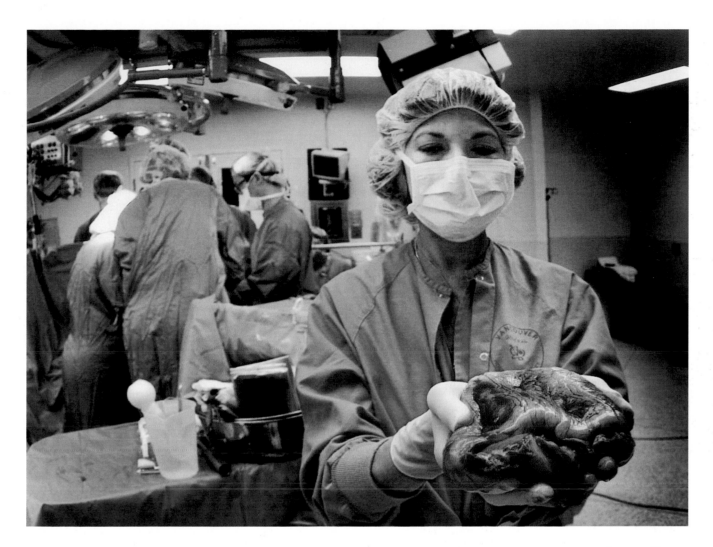

I opened both eyes. I felt no pain, no sense of strangeness that a new heart was beating in my chest. . . .

Like all who have suffered heart attacks, I had, before surgery, been constantly conscious of my heart, conscious of its beat, aware of any irregularity. Now, for the first time in four years, I was unaware of my heart. I knew only that I had a new, healthy one, which obviously was functioning as a healthy heart should. There was no sense of something 'foreign' inside my chest. I did not listen apprehensively to the beat of the new heart, worrying abut how it performed. I found that, thank God, for the first time in years I could forget my heart, and I could sleep soundly.

—"Perrin Johnston's transplant," by Perrin and Peg Johnston, October 1969

On Nov. 17, 1968, Toronto businessman Perrin Johnston survived one of Canada's first heart-transplant operations. Months later he and his wife, Peg Johnston, wrote about the experience for *Maclean's*. The photo on this page shows the enlarged and misshapen heart removed during a 1995 transplant in Vancouver.

87

MEDICINE

HEAD NURSE REMA NAIR HOLDS NICO KLAVER'S DISEASED HEART AS HE RECEIVES A HEART TRANSPLANT
Vancouver General Hospital, 1995

Opposite page
RED CROSS OUTPOST
location unknown, circa 1930

88

HARDSHIP

GEORGE BAKER, LOGGER
Goobies, Nfld., 1959

Opposite page
**RIDING THE RAILS DURING THE GREAT
DEPRESSION**
Alberta, 1930s

Economic depression ran rampant in the 1930s and has struck hard in many other eras. A note on the 1959 archival photo above explains that George Baker—father of five, logger for 19 years—was "returning to William Pope's Lumber Camp because his food vouchers were no longer being paid by the International Woodworkers of America."

Unemployment is the sorest problem in industry. There is a bitter quality in the feelings it provokes. When a man asks for work in order to live and is refused; when behind him are ranged his wife and children whom it is his pride to support by the strength and skill of his honest toil, and he is driven back in hunger and defeat, he would be less than a man if he did not feel himself unjustly treated.

—"A remedy for unemployment: an emphatic plea for the adoption by Canadian industry of employment insurance," by J.W. MacMillan (Chairman, Ontario Minimum Wage Board), Aug. 15, 1930

89

RELATIONSHIPS

PRINCESS DIANA AND PRINCE CHARLES
Vancouver, B.C., 1986

Opposite page
LORD TWEEDSMUIR (GOVERNOR GENERAL OF CANADA) WITH HIS MOTHER, MRS. JOHN BUCHAN
Ottawa, 1936

She looked bored and had a fainting spell, some of his speeches and jokes fell flat and the two were the butt of insults in the Canadian media. As Britain's Prince Charles and Diana, Princess of Wales, finished their eight-day tour of British Columbia, it was not a moment too soon for royal supporters back home. The British press came down hard on the couple's Canadian hosts for planning such a rigorous schedule, which included visits to nine pavilions at Expo 86 and six B.C. cities. . . .

[Hours after Diana had fainted at an Expo pavilion] Charles attempted a joke about the incident: "My wife is feeling much better now than she was earlier in the afternoon," he assured his audience. "And it's entirely due to the extremely advantageous conditions that pertain in British Columbia—the weather and the general fertile conditions—which have ensured she's about to have sextuplets, which is really why she fainted." When no one laughed, Charles hastily added, "It's not actually true."

—"People" section by Mary McIver,
May 19, 1986

Ten years before the most famous royal divorce in recent history, strain was evident between Prince Charles and Princess Diana on a 1986 B.C. tour.

90

CHANGE

ABANDONED FARMHOUSE
Near Strasbourg, Sask., 1991

Opposite page
**COAL MINERS BILLY LUDLOW (RIGHT)
AND GLAYAN GUYCIK**
Cape Breton, N.S., 2001

Mechanization, falling wheat prices and a trend toward fewer, larger farms changed the fortunes of towns such as Strasbourg, Sask. After a long decline, Nova Scotia's Cape Breton coal mining industry succumbed to obsolescence at the outset of the 21st century.

"There was pretty near as many people in town in 1912 as there are now," [Ephraim Erickson, age 92] recalls. "It had three restaurants, two hotels, two banks. Every year it had an exhibition, with cattle and livestock and prizes. There were dances and parties. It was a really busy town." . . . Asked what happened to Strasbourg's formerly bustling prosperity, Erickson answers: "Five hundred farms were bought out, that's what happened."
—"Fields of woe," by Brenda Dalglish, Oct. 21, 1991

Ottawa has ordered [the Prince coal mine] closed no later than this fall. . . . "Coal is the reason our families came here," says Steve Woods, 46, a fifth-generation Cape Breton miner. . . . "It is who we are, it's our identity." Or at least it was.
—"One last whistle," by John DeMont, Aug. 6, 2001

On February 26 [Nellie McClung] headed the largest delegation that has ever assembled on the floor of the Alberta legislature to lay before the members of the House the Equal Suffrage petition. . . . Even the Premier had to smile when she began with a characteristic straight-to-the-point attack.

"You will not tell me politics are too corrupt for women," were her first words and, when the members of the legislature had regained their gravity, for they saw where her argument led, she continued: "And men tell us too, with a fine air of chivalry, that women should not be given the vote, because women do not want it, the inference being that women get nothing unless they want it. Women get a lot of things they don't want—the war, the liquor traffic, the lower pay for equal work. Surely you would not want the irresponsible women to set the pace for the rest of us? Surely no irresponsible woman has any right to force her votelessness on us!"

—"Mrs. Nellie McClung," by May L. Armitage, July 1915

Formal weddings used to make me ache with the poignancy of all that stylized show of trust and commitment. The last one I attended, however, I kept wondering why the bride had that dumb curtain on her head, and why her father was leading her down the aisle to hand her over to the groom—*a man-to-man medieval transfer of rights*. Why was her mother relegated to a seat in the bleachers? Why didn't the bride speak up when the clergyman asked, "Who gives this woman in holy matrimony?"—*is she a fully consenting adult or a warm Barbie doll?* And if premarital chastity is so wonderful that she has to be dressed in intact-hymen white, *why isn't the groom wearing white too?*

—"Is there radicalization after 40?" by June Callwood, January 1973

There's been promising news in the science of female sexuality of late. Very favourable indeed, particularly if you're a rat. A few weeks ago, James Pfaus, a Concordia University researcher working on behalf of Palatin Technologies, a New Jersey-based pharmaceutical company, announced his discovery that, when injected with a synthetic hormone called PT-141, female rodents become overcome with lust—hopping, darting to and fro, and sending all sorts of come-hither vibes to their male companions. Pending further studies—and U.S. Food and Drug Administration approval—Palatin plans to market the drug as a libido-booster for women, to be administered nasally. "Right now, there's nothing in the arsenal for women to treat a desire disorder," Pfaus said. "I think this is the first salvo." To be sure, a nasal spray is not a conventional foreplay tool. But if Palatin can prove that one squirt of PT-141 will get women revved up (in spite of, as is the case for many, fatigue, job stress, perhaps even a loveless marriage) you can bet they'll be stocking up on this stuff.

—"Can science give you a better sex life?" by Lianne George, July 19, 2004

A frequent contributor to *Maclean's* in its early years, Manitoba-raised Nellie McClung was instrumental in obtaining a landmark decision that took effect on Jan. 28, 1916: on that date, Manitoba became the first Canadian province to grant women the right to vote and to hold political office. Saskatchewan and Alberta followed suit within a matter of months, and by May 1918 all female Canadian citizens aged 21 and over were eligible to vote in federal elections. (Quebec, the last hold-out, finally extended the provincial vote to women in 1940.)

In 1973, at the age of 48, June Callwood declared herself somewhat surprised to discover that she had "moved so far and so fast into what is called Women's Lib."

And in a 2004 cover story, Lianne George reported on a surprising—and potentially exciting—medical breakthrough involving rats, nasal spray and female sexuality.

91

WHAT WOMEN WANT

MACLEAN'S COVER
July 19, 2004

Opposite page
NELLIE McCLUNG
Edmonton, circa 1910

92

FUNNY BUSINESS

**RICK MORANIS (LEFT) AND DAVE THOMAS
AS BOB AND DOUG McKENZIE**
Edmonton, 1981

Opposite page
TOM GREEN
Los Angeles, 2004

Endearingly dimwitted and indelibly Canadian, Bob and Doug McKenzie struck a national chord on *SCTV*. In Danylo Hawaleshka's 2004 profile of Tom Green, the comedian's mother shared a surprising fact with *Maclean's* readers: "When the camera's not on, Tom is perfectly sane."

Without their toques, earmuffs, plaid shirts and cold ones, Rick Moranis and Dave Thomas (a.k.a. Bob and Doug McKenzie) don't exactly stand out in a crowd. . . . Fans had lined up at four in the morning to see them at a breakfast sponsored by a radio station, but the maitre d' of the hotel restaurant . . . eyed their blue jeans and open-necked shirts with some distaste. . . . It was becoming difficult to go anywhere without hearing someone say, "Take off, you hoser," and still the two hottest comedians in Canada were escorted to a table as close to the kitchen door as possible, and then promptly ignored by every waiter. Dave Thomas waved politely for some service while Rick Moranis grimaced and waved the smoke of Thomas' cigarette away from his face. "Sometimes it's like being The Beatles," Moranis said. "And sometimes," Thomas added, "you can't get a tomato juice."
—"Taking off with the McKenzie brothers," by David Macfarlane, Jan. 11, 1982

93

TRAINS

STATION AGENT WAVING TO ENGINEER
Mont Laurier, Que., 1946

Opposite page
**CANADIAN PACIFIC RAILWAY
POSTER FROM 1947**
Maclean's cover image, Aug. 26, 2002

Give me a night train . . . gliding through the black when the only hint of humanity in this vast, largely unpopulated country is an unknown light glimmering in the distance.

Then you can feel like a late-19th-century immigrant from the Scottish Hebrides getting ready to open up the Canadian West. . . . Or an ordinary private in the Princess Patricias going off to fight "over there" in the First World War. Or like you've just stepped into a song by Stompin' Tom Connors, Hank Snow, Daniel Lanois—or Gordon Lightfoot.

—"All aboard!" by John DeMont, Aug. 26, 2002

Admittedly, trains aren't the fastest way to travel. But has anyone ever written an evocative song about a short-hop commuter flight?

94

THE ARTS

**PHILANTHROPIST ANNE TANNENBAUM AT
THE ART GALLERY OF ONTARIO**
Toronto, 1995

Opposite page
**A.Y. JACKSON TEACHING AT THE BANFF
SCHOOL OF FINE ARTS**
Banff, Alta., circa 1948

"Products of a deranged mind," "art gone mad," "the cult of ugliness"; these were some of the terms used to describe [the] paintings.

The only possible explanation for the uproar . . . is that we, in Canada, had become so accustomed to seeing paintings made according to a European formula that a simple portrayal of a Canadian subject was incomprehensible to us.

—from A.Y. Jackson's autobiography, *A Painter's Country*, excerpted in *Maclean's* Oct. 11, 1958

**Above, a Group of Seven member
recalls the response to the group's
first show, held in Toronto in 1920.**

95

ROYAL VISITS

THE QUEEN MOTHER ON A WALKABOUT
Toronto, 1981

Opposite page
**FRANKLIN ARBUCKLE'S ILLUSTRATION OF
PRINCESS ELIZABETH AND THE DUKE OF
EDINBURGH**
Maclean's cover image, Oct. 1, 1951

Elizabeth seemed . . . unmistakably
lonely, which won her sympathy;
consecrated to something greater than
herself, which made her awesome;
and touched with shy humour, which
made her delightful.

The Queen had moments when,
unwittingly, she was absurd. During
her surprise visit to a supermarket . . .
Elizabeth examined a shopping cart
with a small child secured in a folding
seat. "How nice that you can bring
your children along," she remarked
kindly, innocently unaware that most
suburban shoppers, on a no-servant
budget, simply have no alternative.
—"The Queen's visit," by June Callwood,
Dec. 7, 1957

Many readers praised *Maclean's*
coverage of Queen Elizabeth and
Prince Philip's 1957 tour, but one letter
writer fumed, "June Callwood needs
further exposure to good manners."

There is . . . a well-substantiated rumour that at least one or two newcomers into the automobile manufacturing field will rush into production as soon as possible with models radically different from the general trend of automobile design which reached its peak of development in 1941. The one most likely to make its appearance first reputedly will be a very small two-passenger car, powered with an air-cooled rear-mounted engine. The second of these newcomers probably will reflect the design influence of the airplane industry, both in its appearance and in the materials used for the chassis and body, with the engine expected to be of the four-cylinder air-cooled aviation type.

—"Tomorrow's car," by Ray Millholland, Jan. 15, 1944

The fastest, the smallest, the most unimaginably advanced—if it looks futuristic it's fascinating. Sadly, present obstacles often slow down the journey toward a fabulous tomorrow. The 1944 article excerpted at left predicted great automobile advances but noted that postwar delivery of a new car— *any* new car—would likely take two years.

96

TECHNOLOGY

CONTROL ROOM, CANADIAN NATIONAL RAILWAYS CENTRAL STATION
Montreal, circa 1943

Opposite page
COVER ILLUSTRATION
Oct. 15, 1940

97

PLANET EARTH

WIND FARM NEAR PINCHER CREEK, ALTA.
Maclean's cover image, Nov. 11, 2002

OK conscripts, straighten up. Shoulders back, tummy in, turn down those thermostats.

This is war, don't you know. Forget Baghdad. Forget Ralph Klein. (Repeat after me: Alberta is not the enemy. Alberta is not the enemy.) We have a planet to save here, to save from the kazillion tonnes of burned fossil fuels we earthlings have shipped skyward to clog the atmosphere and mess with the weather.

Think of yourselves as foot soldiers in what promises to be a decades-long adjustment to the post-petroleum future. The battlefield is your living room, kitchen or maybe the basement where you keep the washer and dryer.
—"Beyond Kyoto: How your life will change," by Robert Sheppard, Nov. 11, 2002

An Alberta wind farm provided an ideal image for a Kyoto Protocol cover. But compared to Denmark and other leaders in wind-generated power, Canada makes modest use of this clean, green technology.

Mercury: Too Extreme
Uranus: Too Cold
Venus: Too Gassy
Earth: Just Right
Mars: Too Dry
Jupiter: Too Big
Saturn: Too Poisonous
HEATING OUT OF ORDER SUPERINTENDENT
H²O
Feyer

98

THE BIG PICTURE

**GEORGE FEYER'S TAKE ON WHY THE
EARTH IS "JUST RIGHT" TO SUSTAIN LIFE**
June 15, 1954

We want to know whether there is anyone like us on some other planet. . . . Or do
we have to go on talking to ourselves—
and perhaps hiding from ourselves on
this same tiny planet—for evermore?

This is a serious question, deadly
serious. For upon the answer depends
much of the meaning of our individual
lives, of the purpose of the universe
as a whole. But how on earth are we
going to find the answer? The belief
that there is life on Mars, for instance,
or that recently we have had some
visitors from some such unearthly place
may be no more than wishful thinking.
There is in fact no real evidence that
this earth has received anything at any
time from outer space except meteors
and radiation.

—"Are we alone in the universe?" by
Norman J. Berrill, June 15, 1954

**George Feyer, whose cartoons often
appeared in _Maclean's_ in the 1950s and
'60s, found humour in life, the universe
and everything.**

99

FAITH

WAITING IN THE RAIN FOR POPE JOHN PAUL II TO ARRIVE
Cap-de-la-Madeleine, Que., 1984

If . . . conflicting religious and philosophical views are to be brought into harmony, the present time is about as late as the circumstances permit. A little more and we shall have hit the rocks for good.

No one of us can tell how to avoid those rocks. But if . . . religion could somehow get us past them, then one thing that could be done by those qualified is to attempt a reconciliation—or, if not that, a broad agreement on certain supreme truths and objectives—between the competing claimants. In other words, one of the chief reasons why religion has no chance to fulfill its function is that it is divided and subdivided into warring sects. If these could make at least some slight attempt at discovering what they have in common, and how they can work together for the continued existence and ultimate good of mankind, a beginning would be there.

—"We must find a faith—or perish!" by Vincent Sheean, Oct. 1, 1948

Writing a few years after the horrific dawn of the atomic age, U.S. journalist Vincent Sheean was convinced that a global religious revival—one that concentrated on common ground rather than differences among faiths— was humanity's best hope in the face of "the imminence of destruction."

Imagine motoring with never a turn of the crank to start the engine. . . . Picture yourself driving until nightfall and then turning on the headlights, sidelights and tail-lights by a simple turn of a switch or lever on the dash, while the car is rushing along at full speed.
—"Motoring without labour," by Harry Wilkin Perry, reprinted from *Harper's Weekly* in *Busy Man's Magazine* (later *Maclean's*) December 1910

I looked in vain for vast hordes of brown-shirted Schutz-Staffel, black-tunicked Storm Troops, and dangerous looking Steel Helmets. There was, of course, a sprinkling of them, but most of the Brown Shirts were helping the police out in traffic directional work. I didn't see a single detachment drilling or marching. Quite a few of the black-tunicked Storm Troopers were to be seen in side cars and motor cars around the Wilhelmstrasse in Berlin, which is Government head-quarters, but they didn't look a particle more formidable than our own provincial traffic police. . . .

I do not believe that there is any sentiment among the German people for war, and I do not believe that Hitler and his associates want it if it can possibly be avoided.
—"The Germany I saw: a Canadian businessman records his impressions of the Nazi Reich," by B.W. Keightley, July 1, 1935

Some startling inventions now being prepared for marketing by Canadian electronics manufacturers will create still another revolution in the kitchen within eight years.

Probably the most welcome innovation will be a machine to mold plates in the size and shape desired for each meal. Instead of washing dishes, the housewife will be able to throw them back into the unit to be scoured and then reground. . . .

Built-in refrigerators will have four or five compartments set at different temperatures, including a drawer for the summertime storage of fur coats.
—"What surprises your 1965 kitchen may contain," Review Section item, April 27, 1957

If it maintains its present rate of development, as monitored by giant computers and mysterious work-in-progress calculators called Critical Path Flow Charts, Expo will open—all the hundred major buildings and activity areas of it, on a thousand acres of manicured grounds plus waterways on a Venetian scale—on schedule: April 28, 1967.
—"How Canada is building (in spite of all you've heard) the greatest show on earth," by Eric Hutton, Aug. 7, 1965

The technology in our future will probably work just fine. It's us we'll need to worry about.
—"The future: will it work?" by Chris Wood, Aug. 21, 2000

The predictions on this page were made over a 90-year span within *Maclean's* first century. They range from 100 per cent accurate (someday you'll be able to start a car without turning a crank) to tragically optimistic (no war with Hitler). Incidentally, Expo '67—Canada's biggest centennial cele-bration and one of the great world's fairs of all time—opened exactly when *Maclean's* said it would. But the unassertive cover line for Eric Hutton's 1965 piece on the pending fair seems characteristi-cally Canadian. Instead of forecasting an out-and-out success, it reads: "Why Expo '67 isn't going to flop."

100
PREDICTIONS

"HOW CANADA IS BUILDING THE GREATEST SHOW ON EARTH" OPENING SPREAD
Maclean's article, Aug. 7, 1965

CREDITS

Photography and illustration credits are listed according to the imagery's position on each page (or spread), left to right and top to bottom.

TIMELINE
Photographer unknown/Maclean's archives; Maclean's archives; Maclean's archives; Brian Willer; RCAF Photo/Maclean's archives; Nott and Merrill/Maclean's archives; Maclean's archives; Photographer unknown/Maclean's archives; Maclean's archives; Maclean's archives

PERIOD PIECES
1 **Future Past** Pat O'Lee/Maclean's archives; Hilton Hassell/Maclean's archives
2 **Plastic** Kenneth Craig/Maclean's archives
3 **Fear** Maclean's archives; Keystone View Company/Maclean's archives
4 **Fashion** Maclean's archives; Maclean's archives; John Sebert/Maclean's archives
5 **Coexistence** Don Newlands/KLIXPIX; Maclean's archives
6 **Recreational Drugs** Maclean's archives; Len Norris/Courtesy of Stephen Norris

HEADLINES
7 **Weather** Paula Penno/Courtesy of Gordon Penno; Jacques Boissinot/CP
8 **Protest** Phill Snel/Maclean's; Photographer unknown/Maclean's archives
9 **Terror** Spencer Platt/Getty Images
10 **Crisis** Peter Bregg/CP Archive
11 **Drought** Glenbow Archives/NA-2496-1
12 **Triumph** Dave Martin/AP; Dave Buston/AP
13 **WW1** National Archives of Canada/PA000556; National Archives of Canada/PA000809
14 **WW2** Gilbert Milne/National Archives of Canada/PA122765; National Archives of Canada/C1700
15 **Conflict** Shaney Komulainen/CP
16 **Epidemics** Lino
17 **Crime** David Bier/Maclean's archives
18 **Controversy** George Pimentel; Christopher Wahl
19 **Fire** Brian Sprout; Paul Chiasson/CP
20 **Victory** National Archives of Canada/PA114617

PASSIONS
21 **Flight** W. James/Maclean's archives; Warrant Officer Vic Johnson/Canadian Forces
22 **Romance** Deborah Samuel; Oscar Cahén/The Cahén Archives
23 **Speed** International News Photo/Maclean's archives; Mark Zibert (Method Inc.
24 **Politics** Newton Photographics/Maclean's archives; Mike Drew/The Calgary Sun
25 **Hockey** Turofsky, Toronto/Maclean's archives; Kevork Djansezian/AP
26 **Airwaves** Rex Woods/With permission of the Royal Ontario Museum © ROM; Photographer unknown/Maclean's archives
27 **Role Models** John Reeves; Chris Buck
28 **Polls and Questionnaires** Terry Mosher (Aislin); Maclean's archives

29 **Cars** Advertisements courtesy DaimlerChrysler Corporation; James Pattyn
30 **Trust** Don Newlands/KLIXPIX
31 **Sex** Jason Schneider
32 **Food** Mackenzie Stroh; Basil Zarov/Maclean's archives
33 **Shopping** Photographer unknown/Maclean's archives; A.J. Casson/Courtesy of Mrs. Margaret Hall
34 **Space** Terry Renna/AP; NASA
35 **Sports (Other Than Hockey)** Photographer unknown/Maclean's archives
36 **The Land** Arthur Lismer © National Gallery of Canada, Ottawa/Vincent Massey Bequest, 1968
37 **Icons** Steve Simon/Edmonton Journal; Larry LeBlanc

THE COUNTRY
38 **Mounties** Photographer unknown/Maclean's archives; Photographer unknown/Maclean's archives
39 **Nationhood** Rex Woods/Maclean's archives; Ron Poling/CP Archive
40 **Great Ones** Photographer unknown/Maclean's archives; Gorm Larsen/The Toronto Sun
41 **The North** Nancy Ackerman/The Gazette; Richard Harrington, O.C.
42 **Canada/U.S. Relations** Maclean's archives
43 **Canadians Overseas** Ken Bell/National Archives of Canada/PA131688; John McQuarrie
44 **Newcomers** Christopher Morris; MacLaughlin Studio, Halifax/Maclean's archives
45 **Statesmen** Doug Ball/CP Archive; Public Archives of Canada/Maclean's archives
46 **Winter** Christopher Morris; Kevin Frayer/CP Archive
47 **Castor Canadensis** BDS Studios
48 **Accountability** John Hryniuk/National Gallery of Canada
49 **Resources** Rob Johnston/Petro-Canada; Paul Little
50 **Separatism** Drew Gragg/CP Archive; Duncan Macpherson/Reprinted with permission of Torstar Syndication Services
51 **Our Place in the World** E. Raisz/Maclean's archives

THE MAGAZINE
52 **Viewpoints** Maclean's archives; Nicholas Louis; Canadian Army Photo/Maclean's archives
53 **Images** Photographer unknown/Maclean's archives; Lucie Santoro; Courtesy of George Pimentel; Yousuf Karsh/Comstock
54 **Line and Colour** Lois Harrison; James Simpkins/Maclean's archives; The Cahén Archives; Photographer unknown/Maclean's archives
55 **Fiction** Hubert Mathieu/Maclean's archives
56 **Facts** Peter Bregg/Maclean's; covers from the Maclean's archives

QUALITIES
57 **Identity** Ken Bell/Maclean's archives; Deborah Samuel
58 **Singularity** Don Hunstein; Maclean's archives
59 **Multiplicity** Canadian Government Motion Picture Bureau/Maclean's archives; King Features Syndicate/Maclean's archives

Text excerpts (numbered in accordance with where they appear in this book) reprinted by permission of the author:

John Barber (28), Pierre Berton (26, 31, 41), Brian Bethune (63), Sarah Blackstock (8), June Callwood (91, 95), Douglas Coupland (42), Mark Czarnecki (58), Brenda Dalglish (90), James Deacon (12, 18, 72), John DeMont (90, 93), Shanda Deziel (27), Sharon Doyle Driedger (22, 85), Allan Fotheringham (24), Trent Frayne (25, 57), Lianne George (91), Warren Gerard (61), Aubrey Golden (10), Jack [John] Gray (75), Ron Haggart (10), Richard Harrington (77), Marjorie Harris (2, 4, 68), Danylo Hawaleshka (18, 86, 92), Patricia Hluchy (32), John Howse (7), John Intini (81), Brian D. Johnson (57, 58, 62), Ann Dowsett Johnston (56), Larry LeBlanc (37), Bob Levin (9, 49), Robert Lewis (39), Jack Ludwig (76 – copyright 1975 Jack Ludwig), David Macfarlane (92), Ken MacQueen (19, 44), Christina [Newman] McCall (82), Mary McIver (89), Mary Nemeth (83), Peter C. Newman (15), Eric Nicol (33), Richard O'Hagan (73), Hal Quinn (40), Robert Sheppard (63, 97), David Thomas (50), Paul Wells (60), Anthony Wilson-Smith (46, 50), Chris Wood (100)

Text excerpts (numbered in accordance with where they appear in this book) reprinted by permission of the author's estate:

Ralph Allen (69), Max Braithwaite (16), Peter Gzowski (35), Bruce Hutchison (36), A.Y. Jackson (94), Creighton Peet (2), Mordecai Richler (65), Alexander Ross (71). The excerpt (94) from *A Painter's Country – The Autobiography of A.Y. Jackson*, (published by Clarke, Irwin, Toronto, 1958) appears courtesy of the estate of the late Dr. Naomi Jackson Groves.

Special thanks
Many people—in addition to those thanked up front in the "Introductions" section—played vital roles in bringing this project to completion. We'd like to express our gratitude to George Serhijczuk of *Maclean's* library for his unfailing helpfulness, and in particular for introducing us to the Libris database (www.libris.ca). Gordon Adshead's *Maclean's* index for Libris (1905-1976) was invaluable to us, and the Libris site is an amazing trove of information about many other Canadian periodicals besides *Maclean's*. A big thank you goes out to *Maclean's* writers and editors Shanda Deziel, Jonathon Gatehouse, Charlie Gillis, John Intini, Brian D. Johnson, Bob Levin, Paul Wells and Anthony Wilson-Smith, who contributed essays to this book. Many other *Maclean's* staffers assisted in other ways, such as providing current contact information for the rights holders of work excerpted or reproduced in its entirety in *Canadian Obsessions*. We were very fortunate to have Meg Floyd as researcher and Barbara Righton as copy editor on this project. Thankfully, each of these extremely efficient women possesses a keen eye, an inquiring mind and a great sense of humour. It was a pleasure to work with them.

Special thanks to Richard Redditt who has worked wonders with our images—they came in varying formats and quality but his keen eye for colour and his meticulous attention to detail has really brought them to life. Thanks also to Peter Bregg and Ronit Novak for photographing paintings in the *Maclean's* collection and various archival material. Assistance along the way was given by Deb Trepanier, Michael Webber, Sean McCluskey, Joe Power, Buffy Barrett, Andrew Tolson, Julie Nicolson, Jeff Harris, Gary Hall, Geneviève Thomas, and Hazel Willis—thank you.

In addition, thank you to Nicola Woods at the Royal Ontario Museum, Judy Boundy at Comstock Images, John Reeves, Larry LeBlanc, Margaret Hall, Don Hunstein, Stephen Norris, Gordon Penno, J. Bowman at the Glenbow Archives, Janet Bridges Cauffiel, Joanne Boulerice at Magma Photo, the National Archives of Canada, Deborah Samuel, Florian Martens at DaimlerChrysler Corporation, Anne Marie Beaton at CP, The Thomas Fisher Rare Book Library, and Raven Amiro at the National Gallery of Canada. Thanks also to Sarah Everts for going the extra mile on research. And to Caroline Ryan for photographing us for the cover.

Along with publisher Scott McIntyre, several people at Douglas & McIntyre in Vancouver deserve thanks for their work on this book's behalf. They include Lucy Kenward, Naomi Pauls, Diane Faulkner, Kym Lyons, Viola Funk, Peter Cocking, Susan Rana and Adam Cummins.

The primary source for material that appears in the Timeline was David North's manuscript on the history of Maclean's, 1905-1970; the Timeline also contains information from *Maclean Hunter at One Hundred: glimpses of the company and its people, past and present*, by Robert L. Perry (1987, Maclean Hunter Ltd.)

—Pamela Young and Janice Van Eck